A-Z of Birds

A miscellany of birding tales
from distant lands

Bo Beolens

Brambleby Books

A-Z of Birds – A miscellany of birding tales
from distant lands
Copyright © Bo Beolens 2013

*A CIP catalogue record for this book is available from the British
Library*

ISBN 978-1-908241-23-8
eISBN 978-1-908241-28-3

First published in 2013 by BRAMBLEBY BOOKS
www.bramblebybooks.co.uk

Cover design by Tanya Warren – Creatix
Cover and book illustrations by Des Campbell

Printed on FSC paper and bound by
Berforts Information Press, U.K.

Dedication

I dedicate this book to my soul mate, the best bird spotter I have ever married, in the hope she will continue to turn a blind eye to my faults and publicly back up my stories, even when she knows the truth!

Contents

Prelude

To my knowledge, I have met Bo a dozen times in the last twelve years. Our encounters always occur at exactly the same time and place each year and never last for more than three days... let me explain. Both Mr Beolens and I are aficionados of the Great British Birdwatching Fair, a 72-hour jamboree for bird-mad devotees held each August in Rutland, the diminutive county wedged between the Leviathans of Leicestershire and Lincolnshire.

The Birdfair, for me, is the social event of the year. It represents a time when old birding pals catch up with each other and shoot the breeze in the full knowledge that their shared love of both birds and the natural world means the conversation never runs dry. Consisting of huge marquees selling everything from wildlife art and optics, to birding holidays to every corner of the world, something the Birdfair also does very well is both inform and entertain the twenty-odd thousand visitors who pour through its gates each year. Lecture tents are always packed as visiting luminaries of the birding world educate audiences on anything from the plight of the oceans' albatrosses to the feathered gems waiting to be tracked down in Bhutan. But perhaps the biggest draw is the Main Events Marquee, where for the want of a better phrase, 'birding celebrities' take part in quizzes and panel games for the delight and delectation of the thronging audiences.

As one of those so-called birding celebrities, my presence on the main stage is frequently required to take part in everything from 'Wildlife Brain of the Year' to 'Just a Linnet', the latter being nothing more than a well-known panel game which has been patently ripped off by giving the new version little more than an amusing ornithological twist. For those unfamiliar with the 'Just a Minute' radio show, the general idea is that articulate and funny people must try and talk for sixty seconds on any given subject without repetition, hesitation or deviation. Any stumble during full flow will be punished by an interruption from a fellow panellist as they then proceed to inform the audience, that for example, they clearly heard you mention the word 'plumage' twice. Any interruption deemed successful by the game show host will then result in both the subject and the remaining time being taken from you as your competitor takes up the reins.

Having been a participant of 'Just a Linnet' for many Birdfairs now, I can't tell you how difficult being both funny and articulate in front of say 600 people really is. Sitting backstage before the four panellists' names are announced to the audience, I've seen some grown men almost cry with nerves whilst others prefer to spend the nervous ten minutes before battle commences evacuating both bladders and intestines.

The first time I properly met Bo was as a fellow panellist waiting backstage before my very first 'Just a Linnet appearance. As a pillar of the birding community, and through his renowned 'Fat Birder' website, Bo was already considered a 'Birdfair legend', and my first impression of him was that of a 'big-boned' yet unassuming man sitting confidently, whilst we waited for the executioner on stage to call our respective names.

Now as the panellists on 'Just a Linnet' are birders first and foremost and comedians very much second, the sparkling wit and repartee at the Birdfair is, to be honest, often only sporadic at best when compared to the original radio show. However, as the game commenced, for the following thirty minutes I could only sit back and admire as Bo swept all before him in a master class that would have left even Stephen Fry or Clement Freud struggling to get a word in edgeways. For the duration of the game the 'Fat Birder' quite literally took centre-stage, as his viper-like wit and an articulacy that only comes by using a dictionary as a pillow, were expertly wielded to bludgeon the opposition.

I seem to remember that I didn't embarrass myself, as I managed to assemble a few points from successful interruptions of the other two panellists and a few lame ornithological puns, but make no mistake, there was only ever one winner on stage that day.

As the bell mercifully marked the end of the game, I glanced at the score-board and quickly worked out that both my score and the other two panellists combined hadn't even matched that of Bo's mighty points total.

And as I reached across to Bo to shake his hand by way of congratulation I seem to remember saying to him in a croak... 'You're wasted as a birder, you should do this for a living!'

Mike Dilger
Naturalist, Broadcaster and a Patron of 'Birding For All'.

About the Author

Generally known to my family and immediate friends by my nickname 'Bo' Beolens, and to many likeminded birders and twitchers as the 'Fat Birder' or the 'Grumpy Old Birder', I, Richard Crombet-Beolens (to give my true name), was born in Brighton, UK, in 1949 and just about remember post war rationing; apparently I used to toddle off to the corner shop with my coupons to buy sweeties. This penchant for all things tasty probably stems from the shortages of the 1950s. That alone is not entirely responsible for my undoubted corpulence. I am by misfortune disabled (a form of arthritis called *Ankylosing Spondylitis* which makes walking painful and sometimes impossible) and, by disposition, indolent. The combination of these two factors with my propensity to consume copious quantities of curry, Belgian buns and, since giving up smoking in 1998, extra strong mints, has conspired to add more poundage. The curvature of my back is an accident of fate, the curvature of my front is self-inflicted.

I grew up in Kent in the south-east corner of England and was introduced to birding by my late father. An accident-prone boy, I dislocated my left hip at the age of nine and then the right hip falling out of my wheelchair in hospital. Needing a passive outdoor pursuit, my father took me fishing, and when a kingfisher used my fishing rod to perch on I was completely hooked (sorry) by birding. The pursuit of girls, and career, and the delights of British beer enticed me away for a while, but I returned to the pastime just too late for the famous 'Tesco' warbler (an American Golden-winged Warbler that was found in a supermarket car park in my home county).

I have lived in Scotland, Lancashire, Buckinghamshire and London pursuing a career as the Managing Director of various charities before moving back to the county of my youth in 1995. In August 1999 I moved to Margate (try to go any further south-east and you develop a French accent) and have been discovering the joys of working a small coastal patch since then.

I rarely twitch (well maybe in Kent) now but still love to travel the world whenever finance allows… apart from various European jaunts I have birded (under my own direction and usually just with the company of my wife Maggie – she loves birding in exotic places but hates spiders) in Australia, New Zealand, Singapore, Malaya, Thailand, Sri Lanka, Goa [India], Hong Kong, The Gambia, Florida, Texas, Trinidad & Tobago, Cuba, Jamaica, Panama, France, Portugal, Spain, Turkey, Montenegro, Poland, Hungary, Namibia, South Africa, Botswana, and Zambia. I have taken 'disabled birders association' (now 'Birding For All') groups to Kenya, Canada, Northern India and Southern Africa. I regret that I also visited several other countries when young and foolish without my binoculars! This way I missed lots of birding in places like Greece, Tunisia, Morocco, Fiji, Tahiti, Hawaii, Russia, and the Ukraine, although I did once take a trip on a tour bus in Tunisia and remember the guide pointing out a huge flock of 'Pink Floyds' in a saltpan.

Between us, Maggie and I have four children (two boys and two girls); in age order they are Matthew, Julia, Suki and Ashley, all grown and married. My son (Ash) is the only birder and is a keen twitcher who has already overtaken me with his UK life list. A fourth generation of birders made appearances in 2000; (Owen started birding as soon as he could hold his binoculars steady… he now even 'grips off' his dad on a walk –

for example, he pointed in the direction of a bird which his father told him was a pigeon – 'No,' he shouted, pointing again – his father had missed a kingfisher picked up by his son!); 2004 (Toby) and 2009 (Bo – she is already a keen entomologist and birder). Jade (Julia's offspring and my first granddaughter) at 19 has strangely been more interested in boys, booze and music. Maggie's son Matthew has no interest in birds but does try his luck in the 'Reality Birding League', thus proving luck is as important as knowledge; his daughter Eve, at 11 years old, already likes birds. My daughter Suki is not a birder despite my best efforts, but she did enjoy the exotic birds which she saw in Kenya when visiting her father-in-law. He feeds birds from his balcony – wild Black Kites that swoop down in dozens to take scraps of meat thrown into the air.

I set up the 'Fatbirder' website – www.fatbirder.com – in 1999 in order to put as many birders in touch with each other throughout the world as possible to encourage friendship and conservation. It has more than 2000 pages covering every country and state in the world, every bird family and much more and gets 4 million hits a month! I also have several other websites about birds and birding – www.birderstravel.com – www.anytimetours.co.uk – www.grumpyoldbirder.com, as well as one dedicated to angling – www.fatfisherman.com.

I have co-authored several books (*Whose Bird* (2003) Beolens & Watkins, *The Eponym Dictionary of Mammals* (2009) Beolens, Watkins & Grayson, *The Eponym Dictionary of Reptiles* (2011) Beolens, Watkins & Grayson) and written articles in several UK and North American Birding Magazines. Lastly, I was a columnist as 'The Grumpy Old Birder' for several years, although this now lives on as a monthly BLOG and podcast.

As of April 2012, my World life list stands at 2603, my UK list at 372 and County (Kent) list at 298!

Introduction

When you look through the alphabetical sections of this tome, some of you may suspect that this whole book is a pathetic framework to hang all my anecdotes on, a farrago and a cynical attempt to fool people into buying a book believing it to be a helpful study of birds.

Frankly I am shocked and hurt that you should think so little of me. This book is certainly not such a transparent and fraudulent pot-boiler – it is all of those things, of course, but so much more too! It is also a way of crowing to more than just a handful of mates down the pub about my birding fortunes. Moreover, I am hoping to follow this book with another collection and fully intend to steal other people's anecdotes along with embroidering a few more of my boring stories. I can do no other as I had the greatest respect for my late parents, and Dad always said to me, 'Son, never spoil a good story by over enthusiastically sticking to the truth at all times. None of the family made it in life by just relying on veracity.'

I think it was George Bernard Shaw who said 'Those who can, do; those who can't, teach.' (Judging by most of my secondary school tutors he was not a million miles from the mark!) It may well be that he who can birdwatch well does so, whilst those of us that caught the birding bug but never managed to fully hone their skills, write about it. If you go out birding, see everything you set out to see, get the ID right first time and never mispronounce a name or call a bird wrong on a sea watch, you may well be among some of the most boring people on the planet. Even if they are not, the chances are that their stories will be. Who wants to hear all about success? It's like all those people who harp on about why the TV news is all bad and 'why can't they give us some good news sometimes?' The short answer is that we would all turn off. Bad news re-assures us that, no matter how many reasons we have to whine, we are bound to be better off than some poor bugger somewhere! It also warns us of what is probably on the way to our door if we don't barricade it.

Since setting up 'Fatbirder' in 1999, I have reviewed, literally hundreds of books. I have read some excellent stuff, but much of what I have waded through has been dross. Some of the very worst are all about how great a time certain birders had seeing birds I can only dream about. On the other hand, I've read a couple of terrific books by complete losers and very much enjoyed some self-deprecating and humorous types who refuse to take themselves too seriously. Hopefully, I will also never make the mistake of taking myself too seriously and certainly endeavour not to make the mistake of taking anyone else that way either.

Introductions are often far too long… this is not.

A is for Anhinga the Snake-bird
(Snake-bird, *Anhinga anhinga*)

I do not have Ophidiophobia, which is an irrational terror of snakes. My fear is rational and reasonable. I fear their venom and do not trust the non-venomous kind because they may be born 'liars' that are merely laying in wait trying to lull me into the false belief that they are harmless. I can actually handle the small constrictors knowing that their muscled bodies and propensity to curl around one's arm is a sure sign that there is nothing more dangerous in the locker. Several snakes are so well known to me and have no known imitators as to be in no way fearful. But all snakes that I have not been formally introduced to, that show no evidence of dental extraction or that do not exhibit unmistakable constrictor tendencies, are not to be trusted further than I can throw them. Mind you, I think, *in extremis*, I could probably throw most snakes a goodly distance.

I am no sportsman, but once, when we lived in an old country cottage, a mouse fell off the headboard onto my head in the middle of the night. Notwithstanding the fact that I was asleep, I plucked the beast from my scalp and hurled it so hard against the far bedroom wall that what was left of its corpse bounced nearly all the way back to me as my freshly opened eyes stared in horrified disbelief. Terror can have an upside.

My fear may well go back to my childhood. Firstly, I, like many children growing up in the 1950s, had a mortal fear of poison drummed into me by my parents. My dad was fond of telling me that a spoonful of nicotine was enough to kill 80 people. Mum made it clear that swallowing hemlock was not a nice way to go… regardless of its philosophical precedence.

I think this obsession with poison was because my dad, as a kid, had eaten Deadly Nightshade berries. He had been induced to be sick and then kept awake for 24 hours in the belief that were he to shut his eyes before the belladonna had worked through his system they would never open again.

I was a country kid, the son of a country boy whose mother was practically a peasant as she kept a smallholding. It mattered little that my father knew most wild plants and would have taught me how to keep safe from their potential harm because for some reason he made sure that my sister and I would take sharp intakes of breath should we, or any of our friends, eat anything that was not deliberately cultivated. While our mates ate wild strawberries, damsons from the hedgerows and gorged on Blackberries all autumn, we spent the time in fear that we would somehow mix them up with deadly Cuckoopint, or, rather than suck the nectar from a clover flower, we would die from eating wild hemlock. God knows how we managed to survive all the field mushrooms we collected because, as my father pointed out, some fungi would kill you stone dead if all you did was lick your finger a fortnight after picking one!

I recall collecting some tiny snakes when we were looking for slow worms. A great place to find them was under the tin sheets left behind after wartime Nissen huts had been demolished. My father looked at the small adders and immediately threw them and the jam jar we had collected them in over a wall. This early fear was compounded when a mate told me how he and a friend had killed a snake at Scout Camp and put it in someone's bed – the prank backfired because the snake crawled away! Once my oldest friend and I were standing knee-deep in a fast flowing stream trying to tickle trout when a snake swam toward us. As we were bending to hold our hands under water, our eyes were only just above the water and so we came nose to nose with this serpent – we just ran. In adulthood I know that the only venomous snake in the UK generally avoids water, whereas the harmless grass snake loves to go in for a dip, so the monster must have been completely benign.

The only other 'close encounter' that I can recall, and which might explain the building fear, was when I was birding in Norfolk as a young man. Walking the dunes, I was desperate for a pee, but not wanting to discommode anyone else, I ducked into the dunes well away from everyone's view. Kneeling down, I unbuttoned and prepared to micturate when suddenly I realised that I was not the only occupant of the hollow – staring back at me, as it were, was a nicely marked Adder or Common Viper. Believe me, in the canon of 'things men most fear' any injury to the part of my body that was, at the time, temporarily exposed, comes near the top. Naturally, snakebite anywhere on one's anatomy is close to the top too... put them together and it is enough to make a grown man flee – which is exactly what I did.

So, I have carried the fear with me for most of my life. However, travelling to foreign lands, which are, of course, far more likely to be snake pits, has been a wish I have harboured as long. In fact, it is really difficult to build a decent World Bird List without actually leaving home. Inevitably, there have been further close encounters.

Strangely, in Australia, the country that hosts the ten most venomous snakes in the world, I have only ever seen one snake and that was in the rear view mirror. I did see an Australian Anhinga there – the so-called Snake Bird – and was wary of walking about to get better views in an area where some of these venal creatures (true snakes I mean, not the Anhinga) might have ventured. Much of my Australian sojourns have been spent looking about furtively in fear, fully expecting a Taipan to terrorise me.

I have also seen American Anhinga in Trinidad and in Texas, and in both these places I have had some closer-than-hoped-for encounters with snakes.

Texas might even be the snakiest place I have ever been. I have seen Whooping Cranes eating Water Moccasins; driving into Arkansas to see them, we passed a snake every 50 metres along the entrance track, and a couple of the other top birding places there were alive with reptilian wrigglers.

As close reading of these pages will show, I am married to an arachnophobe. She is not worried by the venom that spiders carry, she is terrified of the very thought of a spider. That there are spiders on the same planet as her is a constant worry. But she is no coward and, in exchange for the certain knowledge that, wherever we go, I will always carry out a thorough spider survey before she has to enter any confined space, she walks in front of me in case of snakes. Like the companion of a Victorian car owner carrying a red flag in front of the oncoming vehicle, she moves at a stately pace while I cower further back with my eyes sweeping the paths looking for mines. In Texas, her footfalls cleared whole swathes of black, green, grey and brown asps of various sizes. Her selflessness enabled me to see Green Jays and Chachalacas.

In Florida I had no protection – Maggie was riding big dippers in Orlando, while I searched for Limpkins and wood warblers in other parts of the state, so she did not prevent me from getting far too intimate with a Black Racer that did what a Black Racer does and raced across the road in my direction. Arthritis would have prevented my escape, but it had no need to worry as I was rooted to the spot with fear. The racer ran by giving me far less thought than I gave him. Later, when we drove past a tiny Pygmy Rattler, my guide for the day, Wes Biggs, jumped out of the car and picked it up to give me a closer look... I graciously declined his kind offer (or at least I would have done had I not been cowering as far from the proffered beast as I could squirm).

As mentioned, we saw American Anhingas in Trinidad, and we also got closer to a dangerous snake than we should have. We were taken to see a snake sipping water from a tiny stream to be told it was a Bushmaster – the most venomous snake in Trinidad, although it is slower witted than its very painful Central and South American cousin the Fer de Lance. We were told that it was unlikely to endanger us but would slip away more frightened of us than we were of it. What nonsense! I was petrified. The next day we drove past the same spot where the same snake still lay, and it leapt at the car striking the door with its fangs... I was totally safe and totally terrified... as Maggie pointed out, I would not be here to write this if the window had been wound down!

From the safety of a car I have watched a Puff Adder slide across a South African road as we drove from watching waders on a damn to seeing finches in some scrub. I never, ever want to be any closer than I was to a snake so venomous; the thought that we share a planet makes me shudder.

There are two other occasions when I have been close to very dangerous snakes, and both are amusing in retrospect but were no excuse for levity at the time.

I have seen African Anhinga in a number of places, but the first time was in The Gambia – that tiny country, just a short flight from London, is on the same UK time line and was one of my earliest 'package' destinations on that continent.

It is a wonderful birding destination – I clocked up no less than 99 species in the grounds of the hotel we stayed in! It was the first overseas trip we took just for the purpose of birding and found that the cheapest way to do so was to book a package holiday at one of the beach hotels and then just hire a taxi to take us to the birding spots we had read-up about. We did do this but found on arrival that our hotel, like a number of others, offered some birding outings. We tried one called 'Birds and Breakfast', nicely designed so that we arrived at a jetty on the river, just as the sun was coming up, and were greeted with fresh coffee. We then went on board a boat that cruised up and down the river and later dipped into the estuary for a couple of hours. Part way through they fed us breakfast, anchored to a sandbank in the shade of the boat's awning. This was an excellent outing, particularly the bit around the estuary where there were a number of wrecks, moored boats and jetties where many seabirds roosted. There is nothing quite like having three or four tern species all sitting at regular intervals along the same gunwale or series of posts – lined up almost as they do in a field guide – to give your ID skills a boost.

Encouraged by this outing, we booked another couple to places where being in a higher vehicle would mean seeing more than we could from or by a taxi. One trip took us through villages and scrub and into an agricultural area where we walked across fields in search of Ground Hornbills. We dipped out and by mid-morning were taken to some rice paddies. There was only one other 'guest' on the trip, and he and the bird guide were keen to walk around the paddies in search of birds we had already found for ourselves a few days before. As it was already very hot, and we were tired from the hornbill search, we decided to have a cool drink, parked under the shade of a tree while they set off. We happily sat in the truck, while the driver retreated to the shadiest part of the tree to have a smoke.

We watched a bird of prey circling up high in the sky and half dozed in the sun hearing the distant chatter of women working the fields, goat bells and the buzz of insects and bird song. Suddenly our driver began to dance and clap in a very passable imitation of Mick Jagger singing *Little Red Rooster*. We thought he had suddenly lost the plot as his antics got wilder and his clapping more frantic, and then he leapt bodily into the cab of the truck *through* the open window!

We were beginning to fear for ourselves as he pulled himself through the cab window and into the truck bed with us. He spoke little English, but his gesticulations were easy to follow as he pointed to where he had been standing. There, slowly sliding from a ditch and extending several feet into the road was an enormous grey-green snake, fully two metres long but slender, unlike a constrictor. The driver's English was clear enough as he almost trilled 'veeerrrry dangerous' and 'Mamba'!

As the snake sped across the road, disappearing into the long grasses, a group of bare-footed women rounded the corner by the tree with their hoes shouldered like rifles. The driver called out to them, and they stopped their laughter and looked as horrified as us. I don't think my heart would withstand such a daily danger.

During my birding 'wilderness' years I went with friends to the Soviet Union. Most birders will recognise the pattern: You become interested in birds as a child and become a keen birder in your early teenage years, but then the attractions of, as Ian Drury put it, 'sex and drugs and rock 'n roll' are stronger than the need for wild places and avian beauty.

I never lost the love of birds and even managed to do a bit of weekend birding during the first years of my first marriage. However, when work became the focus and a family came along, time pressure pushed birding to the bottom of my internal 'to do' list. Divorce and the confidence at work that comes with experience eventually gave me the time to start thinking about birding again.

I was on the cusp of buying some optics – as I used to get out to the countryside at weekends – but was not quite there when I took the trip to the old USSR. I was hoping to see some wildlife, but as we only visited the cities of Leningrad, Moscow and Kiev, and flew between them, opportunities were limited.

The four of us on this trip each had our own agendas, so agreed that we should each pick an activity or place to visit that we would then *all* go along with. In Leningrad my choice was the Winter Palace, Theresa wanted to see the Aurora (the ship that fired the gun that started the October 1917 revolution), Janet wanted to go to the zoo believing that they had a Giant Panda, and Del badly wanted to see the stuffed Mammoth in another part of the Hermitage collection.

Over two days each of us took our turn. Day one was the Winter Palace. This is the most overwhelming art collection in the world. There are hundreds of superb paintings, amazing tableaux such as a life-sized solid gold peacock encrusted with jewels that was created by Fabergé for the Tsar and many wonderful sculptures. What I found even more overwhelming was that every door was a work of art in itself. This was the one and only time that I have felt truly overwhelmed by the works of man. After some hours all of us were suffering culture overload so decided to move on to see the Mammoth. En route we spotted steam coming from an underground kitchen and well-dressed 'apparatchiks' going there to lunch, so thought this a good place to re-fuel.

The scene that confronted us as we stepped from the street into this cavern was like stepping back into Dickensian London.

Big women wearing white aprons and tall hats stood over massive steaming vats and ladled the contents into tureens. One side of the space was occupied by a huge range covered in pots and pans which were being shaken, stirred or otherwise taken care of by a well-muscled chef who moved as if he was playing a vast xylophone. More white-clad figures stood behind glass cases serving out their contents to queuing diners. Everything in the place smelt and looked totally disgusting!

True to our agreed formula, we all chose one dish and then shared them. As nothing was attractive, we decided that each would pick the dish they thought the *most* disgusting. Del chose some dark raw fish, Janet picked some fluffy white stuff (cheating as she thought it was meringue), Theresa chose a thin soup with a boiled egg in, and I (also cheating) went for a pasty-like dish. On eating, our worst fears were realised, and nothing even threatened to be nice. The boiled egg appeared to have been moulded from plastic and floated in washing-up water, the 'meringue' was more like soapsuds, and the fish appeared to have been cured by leaving it in the sun for a decade or two. As I divided the pasty into quarters, sump oil ran from it and it collapsed into four gobbets of wet sacking soaked in Diesel.

The Hermitage overawed lunch. This was the original collection of the Tsar's curios added to ever since. It was redolent of a 'freak show' with two-headed foetuses pickled in formaldehyde, a badly faked stuffed cat with two tails and so forth. The baby mammoth, preserved by the Siberian permafrost, was the undoubted highlight.

Our evening was spent, like every other during the trip, drinking cheap Russian champagne and vodka cocktails. (There are more than 90 types of vodka in Russia, and everyone packs a punch.) The next day we hurried through our tour of the Aurora, as, in April, the inshore breeze from the Bay of Finland is still bitter enough to cover every surface in ice, and it cut through our western winter clothes like a knife through snow. We made our way to the zoo, braving the begging gypsies and, on arrival, buying tickets from a cartoon Russian granny who sat by a brazier wearing about seventy-three layers of clothes – perhaps she was the original inspiration for those nested Russian dolls.

We traipsed through the most depressing zoo I have ever been to. I am no lover of captive animals even where their welfare is paramount, but here they were merely living exhibits in a sideshow – small cages with psychotic animals in them, like the polar bear that just rocked back and forth and that had chewed areas of its own fur bare. We declined the offer of a ride on a moth-eaten camel. I was pretty disappointed as I had hoped that the zoo enclosures would have attracted birds – free food often does in other zoos.

Del wanted to see the herpetology collection, not because he had any interest in them, but because he assumed, correctly, that this would be the warmest place in the zoo. He got directions by approaching an attendant and wiggling his arm about while hissing through his teeth, a surprisingly effective method despite his lack of acting skills.

Like a lot of 'attractions' at that time, under the soviet regime, you could not wander at will but had to join a 'tour'. A stern-faced and seriously be-suited lady was talking, in Russian, to the half a dozen Russian tourists who were being led around the reptile house, with us in tow. One trailed a young child who for the entire duration of the leader's lectures had been pulling at her mother's arm and crying in Russian. Every so often the mother would let go of the child's hand, clip her around the ear in Russian and then grab her hand and rein her back in. Our eyes wandered as we did not understand a word of what was going on but assumed, by the child's Russian cries, that our guide was telling us all about the venomous snakes that lazed torpidly in the glass-fronted cabinets lining the room.

The child was becoming increasing hysterical and trying to ascend her Russian mother, while the embarrassed mother continued to slap the child. At this point two things happened simultaneously; from the corner of my eye I saw a movement immediately behind the lecturing leader. Without breaking her stride, or even so much as a stutter in her diatribe, the woman continued her lecture and at the same time stabbed down behind her with a forked stick, precisely onto the neck of an escaped viper!

Apparently, continuing to talk, she leant down, grabbed the snake just behind its head and picked it up before depositing it into a floor-level enclosure from which it had probably just slithered! I say apparently, as Theresa related this information to me after my friends joined me outside where I had fled on realising we were sharing our space with the escapee. I was not even aware that I had bolted, scattering the Russians, as fear pumped adrenaline into my muscles.

... in exchange for the certain knowledge that, wherever we go, I will always carry out a thorough spider survey before she has to enter any confined space, she walks in front of me in case of snakes...

B is for Booby
(Red-footed Booby, *Sula sula*)

The islands of Trinidad and Tobago in the Caribbean are both great birding destinations. One country is made up of two main islands that are only 25 miles apart, yet straddle two avifaunal regions, Tobago with its Caribbean birds and Trinidad with a predominantly South American avifauna. Often when both islands house a particular species they are different races and some, like the Blue-grey Tanagers, are really quite strikingly different to the eye. It has another major advantage, that of being a holiday destination with cheap package tours on offer to Tobago and a very cheap connecting flights between Tobago and Trinidad.

The beautiful palm-fringed, white-sand beaches make the islands virtuously synonymous with tropical paradise in the eyes of most holidaymakers. Many people who take package tours tend to spend virtually all of their time at the beach resorts. If they can possibly manage it, they prefer an all-inclusive resort hotel where they do not ever have to venture out from its womb-like folds, so have neither the need to mix with ordinary Tobagans, nor to experience real Caribbean life. Perhaps if they did, they would, in any event, find that men on their way to cane fields or banana plantations usually carry a machete, and this can be a tad intimidating. Although Tobago has a very low crime rate, not everyone on the island welcomes the tourists and their positive economic impact.

I recall being by a stream at first light, watching a kingfisher fishing, and wondering whether the Muscovy Duck on the bank could be ticked, when suddenly, from the corner of my eye, I was aware of a huge figure. I automatically jumped out of my skin, as the six-foot six-inch, dreadlock-sporting, machete-toting local bore down on me. He broke into a broad grin and immediately apologized for making me jump, but I shrugged this off as my just having being taken by surprise, rather than the truth of being, albeit momentarily, terrified!

One day Maggie and I were watching sea birds from a low headline still sitting in our open jeep when we were approached by a group of lads. They wanted a dollar for the 'natural sunscreen', Aloe Vera leaves, that they insisted on rubbing on our arms regardless of our protestations. I offered to give them a dollar if they promised to go away and thought the whole incident was good-natured, even their offer to sell me some 'ganja', which I also declined. However, on Maggie's side of the car something more sinister was going on, while a lad on my side asked for a cigarette that I happily supplied. Maggie was still being hassled for money when an older, more dour lad leaned into her side and very quietly, and in an incredibly intimidating way, told her to give the boys a dollar too. I was blissfully unaware as she just asked me to drive away, but back home, in the UK, one would have called this 'demanding money with menaces'. Paradise is not always as trouble-free as the carefree and cocooned holidaymakers tend to experience.

The newspapers in Trinidad really don't help to create a better image either. They concentrate on the crime that the capital definitely does suffer from. It is no consolation to the visitor that 99% of the crime revolves around gang-life and drug use. We were not only treated to headlines such as 'Local Man found in blood-soaked room' but also a tale from our taxi driver about how a family that had refused to pay ransom to release a kidnap victim was sent the poor souls' head in a shoe box… At the time, I didn't even question the story, however, on mature reflection, I realized that the dimensions of a shoebox and a head are far from congruent... so maybe the tales are more apocryphal than real.

One of my most memorable and wonderful experiences was during our walk back from a wander around a disused airstrip. We had seen several species of night birds, but even more exciting was that we ended our stroll amidst hundreds of fireflies – all at waist height. It was like being surrounded by fairies. Only afterwards did our guide tell us that this was probably not a good place to be after dark, and that the airstrip was still used for unofficial import and export of the recreational drug kind.

Overall, this trip was a terrific one, not only because we dipped our toes into neo-tropical birding for the first time, but also because we saw our first hummingbirds (see H), macaws and euphonias.

We worked Trinidad for just over a week before returning to Tobago. There we stayed in a beautiful beachside hotel, where we could also laze on the beach with Turnstones running under our lounger and land crabs creeping up the shady palm trunks. Moreover, from this totally chilled-out stance we could also watch the birds

There the air was constantly alive with the pterodactyl silhouettes of Magnificent Frigatebirds and with Red-billed Tropicbirds – their long, stiletto-like tails streaming behind as they glided into their nesting cliffs. Here and there were Red-footed Boobies, the gannets of the neo-tropics plunging into the water or drifting lazily on thermals. If you strained the very sinews of your telescope you could just make out some of their brown cousins mooching around the distant islets they call home.

Much of the interior of Tobago is still covered in native bush. Our daily outings found us looking for flowering or fruiting trees to check for Tobago's own versions of hummers, honeycreepers and woodpeckers. The trick is to look for the 'Immortelle' –a tree that owes its name to its propensity to flower at random times through the year, so that there is always one in flower somewhere in the forest. Moreover, it is an instant attraction to the nectar feeders. On other days we sought out the island's scraps of wetland for rails and wildfowl, night herons and egrets (including both Cattle Egrets and Little Egrets that have colonized under their own steam despite the vast separating oceans).

On one day we made the mistake of taking lunch in a super restaurant… not only did it serve excellent seafood and cold beer, but also it sat on poles right over the surf. It proved to be a mistake because we went from chilled-out to positively comatose and, lulled into a false sense of indestructibility, asked a local fisherman to take us out to Little Tobago so that we could get a closer look at the birds there. We could, at any time, have taken a more civilized glass-bottomed boat with other tourists, but instead we went for a more 'authentic' experience. It was authentic indeed, horribly so!

Half an hour later we were whipping across the top of the rollers in a boat no bigger than a bathtub! Our friendly fisherman, posing for all he was worth, stood upright at the tiller, giving the outboard full throttle, while a couple of English boobies cowered in the well of the craft. Like cartoon characters, every time we hit a wave we bounced into the air, then crashed back to the floor with another spine numbing judder. Within minutes we were into the rip tide that runs through the channel separating Little Tobago from its big sister. This was a case of authenticity sacrificed to braggadocio, then triumphing over necessity, because the island could have been approached well away from this terrifying channel. Here we had to ride up and down the ten-feet high waves and, as the land kept disappearing, so did any semblance of British aplomb. Our stiff upper lips went entirely floppy, perhaps weakened by the salt from the ocean spray or more likely from our salty tears. We begged the chap to take us back, saying that we would rather live than perish in the pursuit of a closer look at the birds. Let them come to us, we cried, offering to double the fisherman's fee if he returned us safely to *terra firma*. But the Red-footed, Brown and two Beolens boobies were not the only ones encountered on the trip. That very evening we ticked another... an adult female American booby.

Maggie had just deposited a bag of washing with the hotel front desk, when a lady beckoned her to one side. She was clearly new to foreign travel and asked Maggie what the procedure was for getting some laundry done. Maggie explained that you made a list, popped it with your clothes in the plastic bag supplied for that very purpose, and then took it to reception, arranging to pick it up the next day. No, she assured the lady, you did not have to pay at the time, you just signed for it and it would be added to your final bill. The lady looked a little confused and worried and said to Maggie. 'Do I sign for it in English?' To this day we haven't been able to work out what the alternative would have been. Trinidad also had its share of boobies – many, we surmised, from the same touring party as our laundry lady, judging by their distinctive calls and worn plumage.

The island has some excellent birding places, as well as some very special birds. Perhaps the most famous place of all is Caroni Swamp, because there one can take a boat ride into the swamp as dusk is falling to see the roost of Scarlet Ibis. These iconic birds roost on mangrove islands in the main lagoon and are joined by hundreds of other birds such as Snowy Egrets and Tri-coloured Herons. The mangroves look like Christmas trees decorated with these white and red bird baubles. If you are lucky, on the way to the roost you might see Boat-billed Herons, a sleeping Paraque or the tiny Bicoloured Conebills. In the muddy channels are four-eyed fish, a type of mudskipper, which is able to watch the skies for predators and search the water for prey at the same time. As we navigated the canals into the middle to see the anticipated roost, past Tree Pythons and other wonders, we caught glimpses of the ibis every so often, slowly moving in feeding groups, or flying through the trees on their way to their night time location.

Our boat was shared with some American ladies of the sort that are not unknown on cruise ships and safaris. They were clearly widows and had joined a birding trip more in the hope of bagging a birder, than in extending their avian life lists. Charming they might be, but their interest often wandered, and soon their calls of 'Oh Gee!' and 'How interesting' trailed off as they wistfully trailed their hands in the water, waiting for the trip to be over, so they could get back to the safety of their air-conditioned hotel rooms. The boobiness of this coterie was epitomized by the remark that one of these ladies made to the guide on at least a dozen occasions… 'Tell me again, what's that big red bird called?' As irritating as this was, it was as nothing to the affront Maggie suffered when the ibis feather she was cradling in her hand as she pulled it from the water was snatched away by a non-birder who made it clear by her tone that she was not really asking a question when she said 'Is it OK if I keep this as a souvenir?' However, neither the 'red-bird' incident, nor the 'laundry signature' revealed as big a booby as another experience at one of Trinidad's other top birding localities.

Trincity Pools are just outside of Port of Spain, capital of the islands. These are old water purification lagoons, long since replaced by a more modern water treatment plant. Like many such sites around the world, they are excellent for water birds. Here were Jacana and waders, ducks and grebes and many denizens of the reeds and adjoining scrub. Pied Water Tyrant were a delight to see on the barbed-wire fence, as were Yellow-headed Blackbirds that displayed among the lilies for us when we walked between the tanks. As we traipsed along a new path through the site, we could hear the guide from another group, drawing their attention to some Caiman. We noticed that these small crocodilians are not aggressive, having just walked within inches of several six-footers lying out on the lagoon banks. 'If you look ahead and to the right,' said the guide, 'you can see a Caiman.' One of his charges pulled her binoculars from around her neck and pushed herself to the fore, scanning the sky and loudly asking in all earnestness... 'Is it in flight?'

'If you look ahead and to the right,' said the guide, 'you can see a Caiman.'

One of his charges pulled her bins from around her neck and pushed herself to the fore, scanning the sky and loudly asking... 'Is it in flight?'

C is for Cordon Bleu
(Red-cheeked Cordon-bleu, *Uraeginthus bengalus* and Blue-capped Cordon-bleu, *Uraeginthus cyanocephalus*)

World birding often means visiting very 'out of the way' places, and this in turn means staying in odd accommodation and having very variable food. On birding trips I have eaten some of the very best meals I have ever had, but I've also tasted some of the very worst food too. This has rarely reflected the surroundings or a country's relative poverty, the quality of a hotel or the available ingredients. It's just like at home where a B&B can be a hovel or a palace, yet impose the same tariff.

Most places, at most times, have proved very acceptable but, like most things in life, the moderate, acceptable and mildly pleasant – the unremarkable – tends to fade in the memory. Only the brain-burningly terrible, or the spirit-soaringly superb, can be readily recalled. There are a few meals that I would gladly travel hundreds of miles to re-experience – and some I would run a hundred miles in the opposite direction to avoid. My top award goes to a restaurant where the food was superb but the setting even more so.

For example, 'The Raft' in Walvis Bay, Namibia. When I say 'in the bay' I mean it literally, as it is built on stilts in the sea so one walks along a small pier into its doors. My seafood dish was well cooked and wonderfully fresh, and Maggie still talks about her Potjie – a sort of game stew, but the natural floorshow is what really stood out. At night, lights shone down into the water and the dining room lights themselves illuminated the sea around the huge picture windows. As soon as dusk fell, the lights attracted seabirds, mostly gulls, that came and roosted on the water but were also joined by other loafers like pelicans, and there was the occasional fly-past of a flamingo or two. The real stars of the show were the Cape Fur Seals that dived and plunged, twisted and frolicked, as they chased fish attracted by the light. As good as the meals were, it was hard to savour one's meal when nature was entertaining us so royally.

Vying for top place was at a simple, unpretentious restaurant overlooking Vagator Beach in Goa. This beach is famed for its colony of hippies who party on the beach, but we found the cows wandering among them more striking. I am sure that the prawns there were the biggest I've ever eaten, and they were cooked in the local Goan style of curry. My meals were always washed down with Kingfisher Beer; you cannot help but like a beverage named after a favourite bird. When we visited, two songs were played over and over... the irritating *Macarena* and the Everything But The Girl hit *And I miss you...* I cannot hear the latter song without my mind's eye projecting scenes of the wonderful sunsets over the sea and being totally relaxed savouring the food and drink. Simple food, cooked simply but well, with the open air as your emporium is hard to beat. Give me that rather than the Ritz any day.

A lesser meal, although better than the average, can be had at the Sheraton Hotel overlooking Niagara Falls in Ontario. Watching the magnificent falls, bathed in the colours projected in the son-et-lumière show is spellbinding and lifts the culinary experience way above its star rating.

We had another memorable meal, which I recall ending with a chocolate fondue, at the Seafriends Café overlooking the Goat Island Marine Reserve in Leigh, in New Zealand. Great fresh food is enhanced by a wonderful view from the terrace.

Better still, the café has its own marine aquarium, with a series of glass tanks sporting samples of the local marine fauna, culminating in a dark tank with no life, just old cans and bottles illustrating the problems of pollution!

Of all the meals I have eaten while on birding trips, if there was just one that I had to eat for eternity it would be amongst the least pretentious. You can have 'Village' curry in most places one stays at in southern Sri Lanka. Simple vegetarian curries often accompanied by shredded coconut and rice, crispy matchsticks of aubergine and light, fluffy nan. As I write this my mouth waters with the memory of delicate spices and deep fresh flavours.

We have also had a few meals that, as far as the food is concerned, fall into the 'acceptable' category, but they had unusual and more memorable accompaniments. These include being serenaded in Namibia by the entire small hotel staff, all of whom could have been selected just for their wonderful voices, and having a sudden swarm of termites swamp our evening meal in Nairobi (incidentally, while trying to pick them out of my food, I also found a tiny scorpion that I am sure was not on the menu!). Breakfast in a Lodge in Kenya was made memorable by being accompanied by baboons which braved electric fences to steal food from the tables. 'All you can eat' nights at Charlie's in Cairns in Queensland attract queues down the Esplanade as big as the massive piles of prawns and huge heaps of mud crabs that tempt you to go for a record!

Another simple meal that is way up on the memory chart was a picnic on the pebbles lining the Chambal River in northern India. Here we sat under parasols, elegantly eating like members of the British Raj, all the while watching Plumbeous Water Redstarts, Brown Dippers and Wall Creepers!

Three other birding trip repasts are also worth 'mentioning in dispatches'. In Jamaica we stayed at Mockingbird Hill Hotel, and every meal was something to write home about... dinner of many courses was virtually faultless, but breakfast surpassed any other, they were truly world class. Speaking as someone who tends to have a bowl of porridge or nothing before noon on most days, I was in seventh heaven. Fruit juice and plates of six or seven fresh fruits were mere hors d'oeuvres for a stunning cooked 'English' breakfast with the chance to add Jamaican specialties like salt fish and ackee too. To finish – if you could make room – there were preserves with several types of freshly baked breads and cakes all accompanied by some of the best coffee in the world. There were days where breakfast was an hour or more of total indulgence that even managed to push birding down the day's agenda!

Just once in my life I have had a meal actually pushed birding back by a whole day! I was in Singapore for the first time and wanted to take a day trip over the causeway into Malaysia to do a day tour, during which I felt sure I could not help but see some good birds. The choice was a morning or afternoon, and I had gone for the latter purely because travel had claimed half the previous night. Wandering into one of the restaurants in the very large hotel, I asked what was recommended for a 'light lunch'. The waiter recommended a Malaysian salad followed by spiced crab. It sounded pretty good and not too filling, so I nodded assent and settled down to sip a beer while I waited for my dish.

When the waiter arrived he put several bowls onto the table. One had mixed vegetables, another rice, a third some sort of satay sauce and yet another was full of very large prawns. When

I tasted the fiery sauce that the prawns came in I assumed that I had misunderstood the order – perhaps 'crab' was a wider term encompassing many crustaceans? Clearly the vegetables were the Malayan salad. I looked at the meal thinking that it was really nothing like a light lunch but resolved, after a few superb morsels, to do the meal justice. Alone in the restaurant the staff hovered around me, bringing extra ice-cold beer to soften the impact of the spices. An hour later, just as I sat back feeling quite proud of my efforts, the spiced crab arrived, along with more rice, and several steaming side dishes. I looked at the smiling waiters and the steaming dishes and decided it was not honourable to have the food removed without even trying it.

Tasting the spiced crab was a real mistake. It was, without doubt, one of the most delicious dishes I have ever sampled. It would have been rude not to even attempt the other dishes, so I calmed my palate down with some rice before trying a wonderfully aromatic sauce. The sauce was a perfect accompaniment to the crab, which needed cold beer and rice to dampen its fire… and so it went on. Suffice to say that my light lunch, supposed to be nothing more than a warm up jog in the park, turned into a marathon. Never mind visiting Malaysia, it was all I could do to stagger back to my room supporting an extended stomach with my hands while blinking away beer-befuddlement. It is as well no one had a wafer-thin mint to offer me, or I might well have exploded.

Even packed lunches supplied by guides can vary from the frugal but delicious, to the humdrum. In The Gambia on one of our first overseas trips, the guide was responsible for lunch and just served up rice with an oily tomato sauce – which sounds boring at best, but was, in fact, delicious. One of our South African homestays provided the most delicious picnic I've ever had with cheese and ripe mango slices the main salad components. Having said that, a close contender for top packed lunch when birding was in Australia, there lunch was always accompanied by Lamingtons, which are a type of cake that I became quite addicted too.

Some trips managed to scale the heights and plumb the culinary depths within hours of each other. We birded around Wakerstroom in South Africa, a must if you want to see a couple of the world's rarest larks. We stayed in a small B&B that also offered dinner. Dinner took ages and ages to even start to arrive, and when it did the soup course was so salty it was inedible. Those who actually had a second course were pretty unimpressed and it was soon apparent why – the proprietor and chef were as pickled as gherkins! The following night, after some research, we opted for a nearby inn, just down the road from the previous night's debacle. There we had an excellent meal and were entertained royally by our host (a larger than life Irishman) who told us tall tales over drinks as we waited for his partner to produce the excellent food.

Sadly, I remember rather more bad birding meals than good ones; the very worst food seems to be burned even deeper into the memory. Many meals compete to enter this category but are just not sufficiently bad, dire though they were, to even get into the top ten. An 'Indian' meal in Sydney with poppadoms so greasy you could see through them and 'curry' seemingly based in tinned tomato soup was one. Another was breakfast 'grits' in Texas (although this was ameliorated, both by a friend carving a perfect map of Texas from his pancake, and by the excellent waitress who gave us a certificate for daring to eat the grits). For anyone who hasn't tried 'grits', bear in mind that they are an acquired taste, the closest thing to wallpaper paste I've ever eaten. Just about every meal in Florida that seemed to involve fried batter regardless of description were all near misses on the 'awful meals I've eaten while birding' hit parade.

Cuba has some very special birds, friendly people and a political system seemingly one of the least corrupt in the world. American sanctions over many decades must have caused many problems, but I doubt that this can be blamed for the dire food served in most places we visited. Vegetarians beware, there were days when the only non-meat dish on offer was spaghetti – and I do not mean spaghetti in a delicious meatless sauce but plain, boiled pasta! Despite being an island where it is impossible to be more than an hour or two from the sea, the fish dishes were, on the whole, uniform in their taste and presentation, slightly offensive and unattractive are suitable terms for both. At one hotel the food was pretty good, at most it was very poor, but at another it went beyond bad! I hesitate to describe how the fish there tasted – most were disgusting.

A couple of meal experiences are worth relating not for the food, but because they epitomized other superlatives. One, for example, occupies top place in the 'longest wait stakes'.

While birding in Mexico, we had arrived in the early evening at a pre-booked hotel that looked more like a low security prison than a traveller's rest. None of us could face staying there, not least because it was snuggled between two rather unsavoury bars. Fortunately our tour organizer was very resourceful and had spotted a very modern looking hotel on the edge of town. He talked our way in, and we started the process of checking in with the concierge who bore a strong resemblance to Manuel from 'Faulty Towers' and sported a similar accent. During this he revealed that the hotel had actually been open for just one day.

He gave us keys and told us not to worry about the bags as he would have them taken to our rooms. We all grabbed what we could and took turns to take the rather small lifts to our rooms to wash off the dust of the day. As instructed we quickly made our way to the dining room only to find our orders being taken by 'Manuel'. Every so often he ducked out of the room and it became apparent that he was disappearing to run our bags up to our rooms. Still out of breath he started the process of bringing drinks all the while disappearing into the kitchen. It soon dawned on us that he was also part of the kitchen staff. Every so often he appeared with a dish and with each visit became redder in the face and his increasingly furrowed brow damper. Unfortunately, the dishes seemed to arrive in random order and by the time some of us had finished our meal and retired to our rooms others were still waiting for their soup. Guess who was there to serve breakfast and check us out the next morning?

The 'scariest meal I've had while birding' cup goes to a dinner at a B&B in Humberside. Maggie and I, with my son Ash, had been chasing autumn migrants all day, and, as the day darkened, we became increasingly desperate to find somewhere to stay for the night. Most of the villages had nothing at all, and the few that did were fully booked. On a pass through one village I noticed a sign pointing down a green lane that said 'B&B' and 'World Cuisine'. Intrigued we drove down the lane and knocked at the door. Eventually it was opened by a young man who was the spitting image of 'Edward Scissorhands'. Eerily he never quite caught your eye as he spoke, seeming to be fascinated by a spot just above one's eyebrows. His archaic way of speaking was also as intriguing as the tiny bar we were ushered into. There was barely room for the three of us, and three of the walls were covered in old printing blocks. A notice challenged up to find the word 'Welcome' in ten languages, offering a pint to anyone who managed the task. Naturally, we had to do it and were duly offered our prizes.

When we were shown to our rooms they appeared to be already occupied, as there were coat stands bearing coats in both rooms and in ours there was a toilet bag on the dresser. But the sheets were clean, and, as it was the only port in the gathering storm, we decided it couldn't be too bad, despite the fact that there were no locks on the doors.

The bizarreness of the experience grew as we were ushered into the dining room for our evening meal. Plastic garden furniture awaited us in a room where a swinging cat would have a hard time. I don't recall my starter but remember Maggie having the melon which was served in a strong aromatic liqueur. Maggie asked me to take a taste, as she could not identify the flavour, just as our hostess came into the room. She saw me sampling Maggie's dish and said, in a strong West Country accent, 'You'll be wondering what I've put in the melon!' She followed this up with a spine-chilling cackle as she swept back into the kitchen.

The three of us exchanged terrified glances before she returned with our main meals. When dessert followed I tried to decline, but was told I MUST eat it all up. Like a lamb led to the abattoir I just followed instructions, all the while convinced that we would never be heard of again. I imagined that the meal was poisoned with the sort of brew that would turn us into a frozen tableau yet leave us totally aware as we were dismembered and turned into pies. Whether it was shock or an instant case of 'Stockholm Syndrome', we just accepted our fate.

The evening ended on another bizarre note as we turned in for the night. As I drew the curtains in our room I glanced out of the window to see our host's father out by our car. He wandered over to the shed at the end of the lane and then casually began to pee against the wall... very, very odd I thought. We slept fitfully, and Ash revealed the next day that he had propped a chair under his bedroom door handle to deter midnight assassins!

Years later I was relating this tale to a friend of mine who commuted from the area, spending the weekdays in London and the weekends at his Humberside home. As I told the tale, he paled visibly. He began to question me on the details of the bar, its location and so forth, displaying none of the amused reaction I had always had when telling the story to others.

To add a final shiver to the story it turned out that there had been a front-page story in the local paper. We were right in thinking the rooms were occupied. During the week, chaps constructing the nearby oil refinery occupied the rooms; at weekends they would go back to their families. The newspaper told how a row had broken out between the landlady and one of her lodgers, and she had murdered him in his bed!

Two meals occupy top, or should that be bottom place and, although one involved worse food, the other scored highest for negative ambiance.

For the latter our time on the St Mary River in Australia's Northern Territories takes the prize. I won't embarrass the owners by giving an exact name and location, but it was an example of how to put 'spin' in a brochure. The resort was described as having individual, en suite, air-conditioned cabins. These turned out to be converted metal containers, set on concrete plinths. The shower and toilet had to be accessed by going outside and down one flight of concrete steps and then up another – giving a whole new meaning to 'en suite'. There was air conditioning all right, and it was certainly efficient. You could have it on, but only if you had a strong grip on the side of the bed because the powerful draught would otherwise scrape you off the mattress and stick you against the opposite wall. You could turn it off but you would then stifle in the metal sweatbox with nighttime temperatures around 32°C with the 90% humidity that is typical of the top end of Australia. I swear the air-con unit was an old aircraft engine. This is not just an idle speculation because there was further evidence in the shape of the dining room. This was an old aircraft hangar. At one end was a hot plate that appeared to be a grease storage facility or perhaps a chip graveyard. I think that whatever stuck to the hot plate was scraped to one side rather than any attempt being made to actually clean it. In the middle of the room were a few Formica-topped tables reminiscent of the dining hall of my old school. The food was redolent of my youth too, as it tasted just as bad as school dinners in the 1950s. Come to think of it some of the ingredients might have been around since then as the hot plate fat looked like it had been rendered down from WW2 fighter aircraft engine grease during that late 1940s.

Bad as the meal was it was nothing compared to the company. High up at the other end of the hangar was an arc lamp of the sort that was used to quarter the sky during WW2 air raids. The powerful light attracted several million insects that ranged in size from little 'no see-ums' up to those the size of small pachyderms. As a birder I was, shall we say, unimpressed, but, on the positive side, an entomologist would have a field day – this was bug paradise!

The nadir of all things barely comestible was a meal we half had in Zambia. We stayed at a rather interesting Lodge (see S is for Spider hunter), and on the evening that we arrived were seated at tables wondering what food would be on offer, as the kitchen seemed to be cupboard-sized. When we were assembled for dinner we were told that there was but one starter – soup. This would be followed by a choice of chicken or fish. The soup should have warned us all of what was to follow. I am sure that, were you starving, you would eat the soup. I am equally sure that, unless you were starving, this was not a soup you would finish, let alone order for a second time. 'Rape Leaf Soup' for such it was, is made, as the name suggests, from rape leaves. Rape, being a member of the brassica family, ought to be both nutritious and delicious. I profoundly hope that it is nutritious, because I can offer you complete and utter assurance that it is the very antithesis of delicious. The rape leaf is prickly on one side and capable of sticking to anything it comes into contact with. It has a taste not unlike that of a used, old-fashioned fabric sticking plaster; it is like wet sacking with a hint of Germolene. Maybe rape leaf is best used as a poultice to draw forth pus from a boil. When I say that rape leaf was one of the ingredients I should have said that it was one of the two ingredients of the soup. As far as I could tell, the only other ingredient was lukewarm water.

Several of my travelling companions on the trip had grown up during rationing and would eat bread and water with relish. Frankly, *in extremis*, they would cook and eat their own boots. However, no one finished the soup! Comparing notes with my wife, who had the chicken, it was very hard to see who made the right choice. She assures me that half-raw chicken is an acquired taste, even for dyed-in-the-wool carnivores such as she. I made the rejoinder that there may be culinary arts somewhere in the world that can spawn a recipe that would make Nile Perch tasty, but I find this very hard to credit. After all, how do you make palatable extremely bony river mud? Even the garnish of limp, grey, half-raw fries did little to sustain, let alone enthuse, the diners. The local beer was very good and, fortunately, served as something of an anaesthetic. It took the mind off the meal to some extent… but the memory lives on!

Next morning we watched as the owner's partner struggled to cook breakfast for 10 on a one ring, low powered primus stove that kept going out. I wished I had had some of the cereal before it ran out, because, try as I might, I could not get the forkful of semi-fried egg past my lips. It takes some sort of black art to burn an egg yolk while leaving the white completely raw and as runny as a street urchin's nose. Blessedly, there was an incredible ironic avian accompaniment to these two meals.

Among a plethora of stunning birds from bee-eaters to bush-shrikes coming to the feeders and water troughs visible from the dining tables were several birds known locally as Blue Waxbills. They are known everywhere else as the Blue-breasted Cordon-bleu!

...just as I sat back feeling quite proud of my efforts the spiced crab arrived, along with more rice, and several steaming side dishes...

D is for Dipper
(Dipper, *Cinclus cinclus*)

Dippers are, of course, magical birds with several species resident in the Americas, through Europe and into Asia, with the smartest, I think, being the European in its white-breasted form that we see in the UK. It is the only bird I know of that actually walks *under the water*, feeding from the pebbled crevices of a fast flowing stream. In the UK they are birds of the west and north; often wild places like the West Country moors and the hills and dales of northern Britain. I struggle to see one as I live in the extreme south-east of England, but I have seen them in the very centre of a Scottish city and the heart of a large industrial town near Glasgow… they will make a living anywhere there is a clean, fast-flowing stream. I've been lucky enough to see them in Asia and once 'twitched' an off-course brown-breasted European form in the tiniest of streams next to a supermarket in southern England. If you fail to connect with this bird on a day when you go looking for it, you will have 'dipped' a dipper!

When you first get into birding you naturally want to see everything that the avian world has to offer. At the beginning, for many birders who come to the pastime later than childhood, seeing everyday birds for the first time as a birder is a revelation. The wren is transformed from the little brown bird seen on Christmas cards, or glimpsed in the garden; it morphs into the most cryptic little beauty imaginable. From the virtually unnoticed it becomes a stunner when one is able to appreciate its spots and bars, its stick-up tail or perky looks. The everyday and overlooked Chaffinch, on closer inspection with your new found birder's eye, is not just grey and brown but rusty red, blue-grey and olive hued.

Soon your hobby moves on from re-discovering the birds you thought you already knew, to birds you have never consciously encountered. Mistle Thrushes, Redwings and Song Thrushes turn out to be quite different from the generic 'thrush' of your non-birding life. Finches turn out not to be one sort of bird, but five! Ducks are not a generic mallard mixed with farm escapees but a dozen species half of which are not even there all year round.

Your targets grow from the dozen birds you could expect the 'man in the street' to name and quickly turns into the hundred or so that it takes relatively little effort to see. Your visit to the park in winter is another eye-opener when you start to notice Tufties, Pochard, Gadwall, Wigeon and Teal and see that they have vibrant and iridescent colours through the lenses of your brand new optics! Most birders quickly graduate to wanting to see the less usual and often harder to find birds. Even before you start twitching rarities, you can set out to see something and entirely miss out... sometimes more than once and you have your first experience of 'dipping'.

For many of us some less than rare bird seems to occupy this position all the time. It's not rare, so you ought to see it without a problem, but whenever you go to the right place at what you believe is the right time, it turns out that the bird has gone to bed early, flown the nest, annoyingly migrated or otherwise absented itself. The 'dipped' bird becomes your 'bogey' bird that you begin to believe is a myth or has magical powers enabling it to avoid your gaze alone.

The most frustrating dips of all are those where a return visit by you (if you are overseas) or by the bird (a rare vagrant) is very unlikely. Dipping a dipper on your visit to Devon can possibly be recouped when you go visit your Aunt near Aberystwyth. However, if you miss seeing a Maroon-fronted Parrot on a distant cliff in Mexico it's likely to irk you for the rest of your birding life, unless your luck with lottery tickets is better than your luck with Tamaulipas's ticks.

In my twitchy years I dipped frequently and most distressingly. I hated it with a vengeance. The pattern was often repeated. You would get to the site to find lots of people heading in the opposite direction and begin to ask: 'Is it still about?' The happy birders would reply that it was 'showing well' or 'terrific views down to a few feet' or 'yes, we had crippling views'. Often, as I got closer, the news might change to: 'It was showing well up until a couple of minutes ago' or 'We had excellent views until it went into the bushes.' Further on still, and the faces might be even longer and my enquiry would be answered with: 'We only got a glimpse, then it ducked back into the thick brambles.'

I'd get to the right place to find small groups of those lucky people who had already seen the bird, chatting about its finer points, and maybe a tenacious photographer or two wanting to get an even better shot, among the hopefuls still watching as the dusk gathered, still, like me, hoping to get a tick. Before long we would walk back to the car in the dark, despondently kicking a pebble and mumbling muffled curses. Sometimes such a bird would stay hidden only to reappear after a few days when we ordinary birders had to go back to earning a living. I'd watch the pager intently and every day find that the bird would hang around all week, then, come Friday, there would be no sign of it, and I would have to decide whether to swallow defeat or, ever hopeful, turn up at dawn on Saturday 'just in case'. Of course, I always made the wrong choice. I am one of those people who inevitably pick the slowest queue in the Post Office too.

Hoopoe was a bogie for me for some time with birds missed by anything from days to seconds. Eventually I did manage to catch up with a very confiding individual that arrived in Norfolk one autumn. When Maggie and I went for it we had great views and then overheard a very well known twitcher pontificating to a coterie of adoring acolytes. He pointed out that there was damage to the poor creature's lower mandible. Generally the bird, according to him, looked rough, which was surprising, as it seemed in rude health to us. 'No', he said, shaking his head sadly and reiterated that the bird was on its way out and would probably succumb overnight. The bird did disappear, but not until four months later flying south to breed in Spain. (The moral here is to trust your own judgement and not to be overawed by the reputation of the great and good of the birding fraternity.)

I also regularly dipped out on Ring Ouzel. They are summer visitors that breed on the scree slopes of high hills in habitat that, as you mostly cannot drive to it, was more or less beyond me. Good friends staked them out in the Lake District, and I was told about birds breeding on the moors in the west, but over a couple of years managed to miss migrants and was not physically capable of climbing the hills in hope. Once I even managed to hear one calling across a valley but dipped over and again at spring and autumn migration hotspots near where we then lived in Bucks and nearby Beds. Then, one spring morning, in the most unlikely of circumstances, I connected – typical of the serendipity of birding really (see V). Since moving to the Kent coast, I have seen dozens of Ring Ouzels in cliff top fields when they first make landfall on coming here to breed, and even more robbing autumn hedgerows on their way back south for the winter.

We continue to dip out, but I am now a lot less bothered than I used to be. I guess I now realise that, given my age, physical abilities and shallow pockets, I am never going to see all 10,000 bird species around the world. When we take overseas trips I am not prepared to spend half a day staking out a site for some rather dull, but very rare bird, when I could be seeing a dozen lifers that are as common as tourists in Trafalgar Square. There are birds that delight no matter how often you see them, and I do not find that rarity is in itself a draw. If I was ever lucky enough to pick that winning ticket, my goal would be to see representatives of all the bird families or to see some of the iconic birds of the world I've not connected with yet like Lyrebirds, Sun Bittern and Ibisbill. Having said that, there are one or two birds that I have missed out on that I would dearly love to see, not for their rarity value but their beauty or uniqueness, and because I managed to dip out on them in the past.

On our first trip to India we self-guided with nothing more than a few old trip reports to help us. This means that I walked past a ditch that was then, and still is, *the* place to get a guaranteed tick of Indian Pitta. Had I known and paused and peeked I would almost certainly have connected. This particular gap is compounded by being duplicated years later when I found out after I headed home from Sri Lanka that a correspondent of mine had an Indian Pitta in his garden, ten miles from our hotel, the day before we left!

Another splendidly unique bird we have managed to miss out on several times is the Cassowary. Having been in prime Cassowary territory several times, we even visited 'Cassowary

House' where several birds visit daily without managing to get a glimpse of one.

We have been as dumb at home as we have abroad... such as walking beneath a party of Parrot Crossbills just outside the Osprey viewing hide at Loch Garten. As soon as someone in the hide mentioned them, we ran outside but found that they had gone. Nearly two decades have passed without us filling the gap on our life list.

Of course, the worst dips to tolerate are those where you have deliberately set out to see a bird but have not managed to despite every effort. In the UK, our worst dip was undoubtedly Snowy Owl. Apart from a few breeding instances in the Outer Hebrides, Snowy Owls very rarely grace our shores. In the last few decades there has only been a handful that made it to England. Back in my twitching years one did turn up and over the course of a week got further and further south until its appearance in East Anglia coincided with a day that we could 'go for it'. My oldest friend, who was relatively new to birding, went the day before us and had great views, so we set off that evening with high hopes making sure that we would be at the right place first thing the next morning by staying at a B&B a mile from where it went to roost.

We set our alarm for a few minutes before first light and arranged with our hosts to have a late breakfast after we had been to see the bird. We awoke, dressed and looked out of the window as dawn broke to see thick fog across the marshes. We still tried our best, crawling along lanes with visibility no more than a few yards in front of us... the mists never lifted the whole day, and next morning there was no sign of the bird. It was never seen again. The hole it burned in my life list remains unfilled! Apart from it being a rarity in the UK, it is a stunning bird and an owl, Maggie's favourite bird family.

Perhaps age tempers everything, and you lose the extremes of any emotion as you lose your hair and teeth. For whatever reason, I find more joy now in seeing a new garden tick, even when the bird is common, than I do in seeing a major rarity. I still occasionally twitch, but only within my home county, and can see no point at all in rushing to a bird that you have seen by the hundred overseas just because some freak of the weather has pitched it up on our shores.

...I walked past a ditch that was then, and still is, the place to get a guaranteed tick of Indian Pitta. Had I known and paused and peeked I would almost certainly have connected...

E is for Eurasian Eagle Owl
(Eurasian Eagle Owl, *Bubo bubo*)

My main motivation for a short trip to Sweden was to see a European Eagle Owl, although I knew there were outside chances of some other goodies such as Siberian Jay and Siberian Tit. As it turned out we did get a distant, albeit, a *very* distant view of an Eagle Owl. It was roosting on the far side of an incredibly deep quarry, the deepest hole in Sweden, which abuts the birthplace of Carl Linné – known to the world by the Latinised version of his name Linnaeus – the man who invented the binomial method of zoological classification. But, as it turned out, it was another owl species that gave us the greatest thrill.

We arrived at one of the minor Stockholm airports in the afternoon (one of the 'joys' of no-frill airline flights is arriving 50 miles from your supposed destination). We waited around, finding that there was no one to meet us, although we had arranged to be met by our guide. Being stranded, with no clue where to go, is one of the bad dreams any traveller has who is not part of a package tour, nor self-guiding… one immediately starts to rifle through papers making sure you are at the right place at the right time and looking for a way of contacting the guide for re-assurance. We need not have worried as a young blond Swede hurried into the arrivals lounge and made a beeline for us. 'I am sorry to be late', he said in a singsong Swedish accent, followed, enigmatically, by 'there was delay'. He grabbed one of our bags and took off, so we practically had to run to keep up as he strode across the car park and opened the boot of a battered saloon car. He began to rummage about, manoeuvring his belongings in order to make room for ours. Luckily it was a large space as it seemed to have half his worldly goods already packed into it. We got into the vehicle, but only just in time, as he was already revving the engine, and we almost literally hit the road as he took the ramp from the car park at about 20 MPH over the recommended speed. 'Oops!' he said, as Maggie bounced about in the back seat. 'I am sorry for being late', he repeated, following it with a phrase that was already becoming familiar, 'Oops, I hit a Badger on my way to meet you.' We winced at this sad loss and asked if this incident had ended well? 'Yaah', he replied, 'everything is fine, although, at first, I was worried that the radiator might have been damaged… the Badger is dead'.

Maggie and I exchanged looks of disbelief… could this young slaughterer really be our guide when he was showing such scant regard for wildlife? We settled down having been told that it was at least a three-hour drive to get to where we were staying for the night, and we would travel for half that before we made a slight detour to see our first target bird. As soon as we were out of the city, the forest began and the trees went on and on for the rest of the journey, apart from small breaks where villages broke the monotony, or a few scattered farms made inroads into the forest.

After a while, as much as I love trees, seeing nothing but woodland became soporific, and we were both beginning to nod off to sleep when there was a minor dull thud on the outside of the car. Our guide saw us shake ourselves awake and announced, in his normal jolly way: 'Oops, I killed a Fieldfare'.

As horrifying as was this lack of concern for the wild world, the way in which he drove was even more disturbing. The roads were mostly long and straight and empty, but, whenever there was a car ahead of us, our driver got closer and closer to it until we were practically bumper-to-bumper. It was impossible to nod off as we were constantly awaiting impact. It wasn't even as if he wanted to pass the other vehicle, because he would hang in the other vehicle's slipstream when there was plenty of room to pass by. It was almost as if he was lonesome, looking for company on the long empty journey.

I tolerated this for as long as I could and then made my feelings known. Telling him that I did not mind if we were late. I cared nothing for his chances of getting a traffic ticket and I really didn't mind if he, after we left, was happy to smear his own flesh across the tarmac. What I did mind was his reckless endangerment of the local wildlife and his clients, that is to say us! As part of my protest I pointed out the evidence that he had already killed one bird on this journey. His eyebrows arched as if he did not comprehend and then said: 'Oops, I often kill some birds. But do not worry, they are not endangered nor rare.'

I admonished him further by assuring him that Maggie and I were severely endangered and any damage to us would be an infringement of conservation legislation. I also pointed out that it was likely to result in damage to him if I was cornered! Our guide became a bit more subdued, but not for long, soon he was telling us all about other trips he had led.

When we travelled to the northern-most point of our tour we were bitten to pieces by mosquitoes, while trying to get a glimpse of some Siberian Tits. We retreated to a café and enjoyed an ice cream in the sunshine during which we had a distant flyby Siberian Jay, the only one we saw. This prompted a story from our guide about how he had struggled through the snow to show someone Siberian Jays – the species they most wanted to see. He went to each of the local spots he knew about, including several specially placed feeders where he had watched jays for many hours. Everywhere they went they 'dipped out' on the birds. They saw lots of great birds but never connected with the Jays and eventually had to leave for home still disappointed. The guide finished his tale and looked wistful then said: 'I didn't have the heart to tell them. On the way to pick them up at the airport, oops, I felt a thud against the car. I never managed to scrape all the remains from the radiator grill. All through the trip a Siberian Jay was stuck to the car!'

We saw some great birds during our few days enjoying the Swedish spring. Day one's break after 90 minutes on the road was at a triangle of scrubby woodland where roads crossed close by an industrial site. This mucky little scrap of land was alive with the song of Common Rose Finches, but even I could tell something else was singing too... then the bird flew to the edge of the muddy, osier-ringed ditch into plain view, my first, and so far only, Blythe's Reed Warbler – the very bird we had made this diversion to see. Elsewhere we birded into the early hours of the morning, a novel experience on our first visit to 'the land of the midnight sun'. Up on a bare plateau by the Norwegian border we experienced the Nightingale-like songs of Bluethroats, watched Red-necked Phalaropes spinning on pools and spotted the nest of a Pomarine Skua.

During one of the drives Maggie suddenly exclaimed that she could see Sand Martins nesting. The guide explained that she must be mistaken, as there were no colonies in the area. Very reluctantly, and at Maggie's insistence, he retraced the last mile and, sure enough, through a gap in the trees we all saw a clearing where land had slipped to leave a tall clay bank that was alive with Sand Martins. The guide ran into the clearing and started counting the nests then, as he walked back to the car, we could hear him talking on his cell phone... he explained to us that he was telling an ornithologist friend that *he* had discovered a new Sand Martin colony that had never been surveyed. I don't know why this surprised us. This was neither the first, nor the only time that we have encountered a guide who first dismissed an observation and then later claimed it as his own!

On another evening we drove to the top of a pass where reindeer roamed and snow was still cladding the hollows, creating a patchwork that sometimes hid and sometimes disclosed Ptarmigan. As we watched a moose moving along the edge of the tree line, a Gyr Falcon flashed into view, and we marvelled at its speed as it disappeared over the hills. On one day out we saw pool after pool, each hosting a Black-throated Diver or two and sometimes a pair of Spotted Redshank. But the top bird of the trip was another owl.

On our last day we had planned to drive back to Stockholm because we had an early flight the next morning. Our guide had a friend, a woodsman, who, he said, had placed nesting boxes around for Hawk Owls, and he was just off the route we needed to drive down to Stockholm. So it was that we turned off the main road and after a short while left the tar-seal, and the guide drove us miles down an unmetalled forest track. We stopped at a typical Swedish house with a sharply angled roof designed to shed snow. There the guide chatted with a friendly guy who spoke no English but told our guide that one of his nest boxes was occupied and the chicks were already ringed. He gave directions, and we set off even deeper into the forest.

After some miles the guide slowed the car, explaining that we were getting close now, and he did not want to miss the marker that his friend had left for him. Eventually he parked the car and pointed through the forest to where we could make out that there was a depression with some cleared timber and still standing, but dead trees. He beckoned us to follow him.

This turned out to be a great deal harder than we expected. Here the forest was nothing like any that I have experienced elsewhere. The ground was extremely uneven with everything covered in really thick moss. Take one step forward and you would sink to the knees in mud, try to move forward and your foot would slide across a mossy rock and then, if you were not careful, you would be pitched into a six-foot pit barely visible through the under-storey and sponge-like mosses.

We had to clamber over huge fallen timbers, fight against the whip-like low branches and all the while be in fear of a soaking or breaking a bone on the massive boulders. The guide leapt ahead, used to the terrain, while we struggled to inch our way forward. Eventually, we found our way to a slight ridge from which we overlooked the depression with the nest site. At this point the guide came back to us.

'I will go and bring you a chick,' he said. We told him as forcefully as we could that under no circumstances was he to disturb the birds on our behalf, and that the chicks' welfare was paramount. He moved off towards a dead tree we could see in the clearing. As he neared it, first one parent owl and then the other took off from their hiding places and into the branches of a nearby tree, starting to call loudly. We enjoyed the wonderful views of the Hawk Owls that this afforded, then called out to the guide, pleading with him to leave them well alone and letting him know that we were returning to the car. Despite the fact that it took us a long time to work our way back to the car, although it was close and in sight, it was a further age before the guide re-appeared. We had begun to wonder if he had lost his footing in the difficult land and injured himself. Then, suddenly, he burst from the forest along the track and jogged towards the car clutching his head. By the time he reached us he seemed almost to be in tears.

'Is there blooding?' he asked, leaning forward to reveal the deep scratches on his scalp. He explained in a tremulous voice that, as he lifted a chick from the nest in the hollow tree, the female had attacked him. He quickly put the chick back, but, before he could retreat, the male had joined in too. They 'dive bombed' him several times as he tried to get back to the shelter of the trees, each time raking their talons through his hair. Naturally, we made very sympathetic noises and reassured him that the injuries were superficial. He would soon be OK, we told him as he began the long drive to the airport. Every so often he pulled at the rear-view mirror and strained to get a glimpse of his head wounds. Of course, inside, we were both imagining the Hawk Owl saying to itself in owl speak... 'Ooops, I killed a bird guide!'

'Oops, I often kill some birds. But do not worry, they are not endangered nor rare'...

F is for Florida Scrub-jay
(Florida Scrub-jay, *Aphelocoma coerulescens*)

When 'she who must be obeyed' announced that we were taking our daughter and granddaughter to Florida to 'do' Disney and 'Universal Studios', my heart sank faster than a stooping peregrine! Some things fill me with greater horror, but they all involve personal injury. I had to sit down with a calming cup of tea – trying to reconcile visiting a bird-rich area with being City bound, rubbernecking at manmade sites or strapping myself to a vomit-inducing ride rather than rising early to sneak up on snipe and stalk storks. Something drastic had to be done!

I considered options like throwing myself down the stairs or slipping something debilitating, but non-fatal, into the wife's dinner. But at that time we lived in a bungalow, and I'd really miss the bird-spotting skills of my better half, besides I'm quite fond of the old girl. I tried whining, pleading and crying, but nothing worked, so I compromised... I'd fly to Florida, but we would have to stay in a hotel with wireless Internet so I could work in our room to raise money to pay for the trip! I searched the web and posted a message on FLBirds and BRDBRAIN:

> *Calling Orlando birders – I'm a UK birder coming to Orlando in March – my family will be spending all my money at various attractions, while I stay in my hotel with my laptop trying to pay for the trip :-) I am wary of driving, so need rescuing for a few day trips birding – if anyone fancies picking me up from International Drive and show some Florida specials to a Brit, I'd be*

happy to pay for gas and lunch! My website is pretty well-known; used by about 150,000 birders a month, so I could return the favour to Florida birders wanting to bird in the UK when they bring their family over to see my local town (Canterbury) with its 1,000 year-old cathedral etc.. bo beolens aka The Fat Birder

I knew I would get some positive responses. Say what you like about Americans (and much of the rest of the world does), but they can be the most generous folk in the world, and birders like nothing more than sharing their hobby. Luckily I've had a couple of North American trips, so have an ABA list, but it did, and does, have plenty of gaps to fill. Within a week I had had several positive responses, which meant I could plan five full-on birding days interspersed with 'rest days' to answer emails, update websites and remove the wrinkles from my bones.

Cheri Pierce offered to take me into Orlando Wetlands where she could drive this arthritic old birder around the lagoons. Gallus Quigley would take a day off from his job as a Park Ranger to show me Merritt Island National Wildlife Reserve (NWR); Jean Williams offered a drive to the west coast hoping for migrants, and still other birders would show me Three Lakes. I began to plan for Florida's special birds... who could find a Florida Scrub-Jay for me and who would show me my first Limpkin, where would Red-cockaded Woodpeckers leap into view before my scope? Then came the call from Florida's top lister and most experienced professional bird guide, that verbal hurricane Wes Biggs! As I swapped email addresses, birding anecdotes and political opinions with this anglophile, I knew I'd met a fellow spirit; someone that, had arthritis not shrunken my spine, would have made a perfect set of bookends with me, as he is a hairy old hippy and his girth, like mine, is nearly as big as his reputation!

There were two days between our arrival and my first outing, which proved blessedly fortuitous. The 'package' holiday had included 'premium' class flights, but it turned out that all this meant was that we had merely paid extra for 'free' food; there was no more legroom than in ordinary economy'! Nine hours with my knees and nose (courtesy of my curved spine) jammed to the seatback in front resulted in me being confined to bed for the first two days in the sun, and my Florida list was confined to House Sparrow, Cardinal, Turkey Vulture and White Ibis – all as 'window ticks'.

The Great Florida Limpkin Hunt

After two days mostly lying flat recovering from the flight, I was waiting outside the hotel lobby at 'silly' o'clock in the morning in unseasonably cool, windy weather when Cheri Pierce arrived. Unexpectedly, Wes accompanied her! He immediately explained that he was determined to find me more birds for me than anyone else, so had invited himself on *all* my planned outings. I had an irrepressible and sneaking suspicion that it was really to get me to buy him breakfast all week long! Being hairy is not the only thing Wes shares with hobbits; he is also fond of breakfast and happy to have several at any time of the day.

First stop was Orlando Wetlands Park where Limpkins abound and King Rails are known to walk in front of the car. It is a terrific site... hundreds of acres of lagoons, woodland and grassland, which effectively filters Orlando's wastewater. The very first lagoon set the scene with its mosaic of water plants holding a myriad of herons and waterfowl, and the grassy enclosing bunds hiding skulking Savannah Sparrows and Palm Warblers. The only fly in Florida's ointment was a strong, cold wind that was not only keeping birds from showing but also freezing the kidneys off a Brit dressed only in a thin T-shirt and shorts that he mistakenly thought appropriate for Florida weather.

Nothing threatened to add itself to my life list, but it was, as Americans say, 'neat' to see the Great Blue and Little Blue Herons, Least Bitterns and Purple Gallinules strutting their stuff in the bright sunshine, Rough-winged Swallows vacuuming the sky clean of insects and shorebirds probing the waters edge for worms and molluscs. A scattering of early migrants sang in the trees, and a top bird for the area, the Short-tailed Hawk, soared overhead, but the Rails and Limpkins were all in hiding – perhaps they too had dressed for a Florida Spring and were skulking somewhere warm.

By consensus we moved on to Tosohatchee Wildlife Management Area where the trackside ditches down to the St John's River hold Limpkins, and the pine trees house Bachman's Sparrows. On route, Cheri stopped on Taylor Creek Road when she spotted a Swallow-tailed Kite – three Swallowtails soared over the tree line – my first trip lifer and surely one of the world's most attractive raptors! Tosohatchee is a great site, but its ditches did not give up Limpkins… just warblers in woodland, 'gators and pond turtles sunning themselves in the waterways and bluebirds prospecting all the birdhouses that had been attached to the power pylons that paralleled the road down to the river.

We adjourned to a 'Subway' outlet for a Limpkinless lunch, over which Cheri and Wes discussed options and decided that our next stop would be Viera Wetlands (a water treatment works once more but on a much smaller scale) where King Rail and Limpkin usually abound. We drove around the dykes and impoundments ever hopeful, managing some new ducks for the day and admiring the ever-present Red-winged Blackbirds and other common delights. We even heard Limpkins, but sadly they still did not show themselves.

This is typical of the joys of showing visiting birders your favourite hot spots. I've often done it myself – you take your new friend to birding spots where, ninety-nine times out of a hundred you get the target birds practically eating from your hand, only to find that this is the 100th time and you draw a blank. The thing is, the visitor doesn't mind at all, 90% of what they see will be lifers or birds they've rarely seen. You, of course, are distraught, feeling that you are letting down the visitor, your country and even the World Ornithological Congress!

So, a happy Bo lapped up the Loggerhead Shrikes, drooled over Dowitchers and loved Lesser Scaup, while my guides sobbed into their subways and hid embarrassment behind hotdogs.

Wes was not daunted, indeed I doubt Wes has ever been daunted, daunting maybe, but daunted? Never!

'Right,' he said, as we drove toward Brinson Park in Kissimmee [which I now know is pronounced kiss-IMMEE not KISS-immee]. 'We will see a Limpkin within two minutes forty-eight seconds of arriving!'

As it happens he was way out. It was well over three minutes after arriving that, on raising my bins, I spied a Limpkin limping into view... within the next four minutes I had seen my second and third and added the not inconsiderable bonus of my first, and so far only, Snail Kite! Thus ended my first outing of the trip with three life birds, a growing Florida list and a big smile on my face.

The next outing was planned to be the pinnacle of my sojourn. Searching for a Scrub-Jay was at the top of my wanted list, as this is the State's only endemic, and who knows if I'll ever return to Florida.

After another necessary restorative day I met Wes at 'even sillier' o'clock on a windless day, and we headed toward Zellwood and the wetland restoration area near Lake Apopka. En route we picked up breakfast then drove to Duda Road where Wes called in life birds numbers four and five: Barred Owl and a Chuck-wills-widow. We celebrated over breakfast serenaded by the dawn chorus of Carolina Wrens, Gray Catbirds and Great Crested Flycatchers. Wes heard a distant Great Horned Owl that we scoped for and found silhouetted against the dawn. Then we moved on to Ranch Road near Astatula where Wes duly delivered one of the top trip highlights.

Along the sandy road through scrub we had great views of three woodpecker species, as well as Northern Bobwhites and Blue Jays, all the time having a background chorus of titmice and wrens. Wes asked me how many Florida Scrub-Jays I would like to see? He imitated calls until a family of five appeared and I watched in awe as they fed from his outstretched hand… then one landed on mine to take a peanut! 'Brilliant' as we Brits say (or to quote Wes's impersonation 'Bwillyant'). What could be better than an endemic 'lifer' eating out of your hand?

It's true what George Bernard Shaw said of the US and UK – they really are two nations separated by a common language. I guess we are used to American TV shows using terms and making references that mean nothing to us – often from the arcana of baseball or the esoteric world of American football. It comes as a shock when words we use everyday furrow the brow of the listener. 'Brilliant' just means shining like a jewel in American rather than the generic terms for all things 'terrific' that is has come to mean in English English.)

One might think that the day could only go down hill from there? Not a bit of it! We spent several hours in the restoration area… where land is being restored to natural habitat after the overuse of agricultural chemicals was responsible for massive accidental slaughter. Despite its history it's a wonderful wetland wildlife area, high in bird variety and density. I saw more Ospreys here than all those I've ever seen on five different continents put together! As I peered into an alligator-filled lagoon, all five of the adjacent power poles were topped with Ospreys, each eating a fish (of several different species). Here were Swamp Sparrows and Barn Swallows, Red-shouldered Hawks and the season's first Chimney Swifts; we even heard King Rails three feet away from us but never managed to glimpse these elusive denizens of damp ditches.

Wes headed to his friend Doug Stuckey's house in Titusville where Painted Buntings dutifully visited feeders for us. These were not only welcome in themselves but doubly so as I had dipped this species by mere seconds when visiting Pelee in Ontario some years before. There is nothing quite like filling a gap in the list created by 'the one that got away'. After another stop at the Lake Lizzie Nature Preserve east of St Cloud for the most attractive Red-headed Woodpecker (Maggie always says I'm a sucker for a Redhead) and Eastern Towhee, we headed onwards for Red-cockaded Woodpecker and Brown-headed Nuthatch with the added bonus of the scarce (for Florida) Hairy Woodpecker – turning the day into a 7-woodpecker day – and a fly- over by two, even rarer, White-tailed Kites.

The day had been awash with top birds but was not over until we had driven down Joe Overstreet Road north of Three Lake Wildlife Management Area between cattle pastures, looking for Burrowing Owls. Despite Wes's attempt to convince me that a heap of cow dung was indeed a Burrowing

Owl, I eventually spotted the real thing. These wished-for beauties warranted a shy manly hug from me – just about as demonstrative as an Englishman can be! The only downer of that day was finding a freshly killed Crested Caracara on the road home (now in the collection of the University of Central Florida).

Bachman's Sparrows & Blue-Gray Time-wasters

My third outing was with Gallus Quigley who first took us to Lori Wilson Park. This small reserve near Cocoa Beach is a migrant trap, and, while there had not been a significant fall, it was still terrific to be quietly watching as more and more warblers moved through the trees to the drinking pool while Catbirds and Painted Buntings visited the feeders. This spot produced a number of life birds for me, including Worm-eating Warbler and Cape May Warbler, and several birds that we did not see anywhere else, such as Prairie Warbler and Tennessee Warbler.

Next we drove to Gallus's second home, Merritt Island National Wildlife Reserve, where we still failed to connect with rails, but I did get another lifer in the shape of a fine-looking Stilt Sandpiper. This more than compensated me by helpfully associating with Lesser Yellowlegs and Dowitchers, so that I could compare distinguishing features. I also saw my second ever Willet. This was a different sub-species to the one that I had seen in California – a new 'subbie' tick. It made me realise that I was seeing many new races, and that I would have to carefully check out what I had seen where when I got home.

After lunch we headed again for Tosohatchee Wildlife Management Area, and this time we did connect with Bachman's Sparrows... by virtue of Wes's playing tapes, the wind had dropped and because of Gallus's familiarity with a species whose conservation he had worked on for years.

We drove down to the St John's River and then worked the track back stopping to search the woodland edge for warblers. At home I can pick up LBJs, the cryptic and mostly dull olive-green warblers that we get in the UK, even against olive-coloured leaves, but in Florida, to my dismay, I had difficulty with colourful warblers, even when they were pointed out to me. Gallus homed in on any passerines finding that most were the same species, Blue-Gray Gnatcatchers or, as he called them, 'Blue-Gray Time-wasters', because so often, initially, they seem to be something more interesting.

A raptor drifted overhead. My guides identified it after a cursory glance as a Swallow-tailed Kite. Confused I pointed out that its tail was not swallow-like. Their closer inspection revealed a great find, Mississippi Kite! It shows that even experts – and believe me these two are among the best birders I've had the privilege to raise my field-glasses to – can overlook the unexpected when trying to get a dumb foreigner onto some easy birds!

Here We Go Round the Mulberry Bush

My final two outings were to Florida's west coast in search of migrants. First Jean Williams kindly drove Wes and me to St Petersburg and around Tampa Bay, and on a second occasion Wes took me back to the coast for other goodies.

On the first day we found no Wilson's Plovers by the Sunshine Skyway Bridge Approach but connected with Monk Parakeets nesting in floodlights at Eddie Moore Park in Safety Harbor and Black-hooded Parakeets at Fort DeSoto where we also had a fly-over Frigatebird. Here incoming warblers joined a large Cedar Waxwing flock at a renowned birding tree. It was excellent to see Indigo Bunting, Scarlet and Summer Tanager, Orchard Oriole, American Redstart and assorted warblers. We checked out the famously good migrant attractor, the Mulberry Tree next to the Park Manager's house, only finding Orioles and Catbirds. The day ended with a drive around Jean's favourite localities – Tenoroc Fish Management Area and Saddle Creek Park. It was easy to see why she favoured them, warbler trees, a roost of Black Vultures and some very obliging Limpkins too!

Even my final day gave up lifers. Wes found Wilson's Plovers at the East Beach turn around and Yellow-billed Cuckoo at the North Beach woods back at Ft DeSoto, as well as other birds for my Florida list, and I finally ticked Yellow-throated Warbler at John Chestnut Sr Park on Lake Tarpon.

It's difficult to overemphasise how hard these guys worked to get a complete stranger with limited mobility up close and personal with avian delights. One day I'll steal Wes's best anecdotes and turn them into my own. It's a shame I cannot share any of Wes's rants about people who let cats roam or the myth of the Ivory Bill; I don't think I could change names sufficiently to protect myself from lawsuits!

I finished with a Florida list of 159 species, 23 lifers and four new friends; not bad for a trip I never wanted to take!

…Despite Wes's attempt to convince me that a heap of cow dung was a Burrowing Owl, I eventually spotted the real thing…

G is for Goose
(Goose, *Anatinae*)

Tiritiri Matangi is an island in Auckland Bay in New Zealand, its name means 'tossed by the wind'. It is just about a mile long and only half as wide, and it was farmed for many years after most of the native bush (94%) had been cleared back in colonial times. It was chosen as a place to re-populate with native flora and fauna as, being an island, it was relatively easy to eliminate all the non-native predators... something that happened as one of the first initiatives by 'Forest & Bird' (i.e. Royal Forest and Bird Protection Society of New Zealand)... to make safe havens for native New Zealand species.

Polynesian rats, stoats and weasels can devastate populations of flightless or poor-flying birds, and goats, pigs, possum and deer often out-compete native taxa for limited foods. So these competitors also need to be removed in order for native flora and fauna to thrive. (Competition is a phenomenon that is often overlooked by conservationists. We amateur birders tend to assume that the threats are predators who want to eat the birds we want to preserve, whereas, more often than not, they are far less of a problem than non-predators that take over the niche more properly occupied by our preservation target species.)

Luckily, with islands it is relatively easy to keep predators from invading again, especially if visiting is strictly limited, which it is on Tiri – there is just one building for the warden and volunteers (apart from the automated lighthouse), and only organized groups can land. Moreover, they must take away with them whatever they bring. However, food waste is composted, and there are composting toilets that have been trouble free for a generation, and even the bunkhouse and shop are sun-powered.

Through careful management many non-native plant species have been eliminated. Native bush has, over the last several decades, grown up or been replanted, and the island is fringed with tree ferns and palms and so forth. Just like a 'set-aside' field in the UK, if you leave the land alone, age-old seeds will germinate and plants will struggle to the surface that haven't seen the light of day for years, having been chewed to the roots by domestic stock or feral foreign fauna. However, after 120 years of grazing, Tiri was struggling to re-clothe itself and had to be given a helping hand because every natural seedling on the island had been gnawed down by Kiore Rats, and rank farmland grasses smothered any re-growth. From the mid-1980s until the mid-1990s nearly 300,000 trees were planted!

When you land on the island you walk along the jetty to the beach, and there is a steep track up to the warden's place where they have a tiny gift shop and café – although all it serves is tea and coffee, it does provide plastic picnic tables and chairs – the sort with holes in the seats so that rainwater drains off.

On one side of the island is a boardwalk with steps every so often as it slowly meanders, gently ascending the steep sides of the island, up to the plateau where there is still a clearing. Every so often, through gaps in the taller trees, one can glimpse a fine vista across Auckland bay. Periodically you reach one of the very handily placed benches, where you can rest up and enjoy the views and the sight and songs of the native birds that now abound. A cleverly designed handrail also serves as a drinking trough, so, if you sit quietly, the native parrots, pigeons and passerines sip water just feet away and at eye-level, and all around you are the sounds that were so familiar to early settlers but are sadly absent from much of the mainland in modern times.

If you take a small piece of polystyrene with you, you can attract many of the passerines. Just wet your watch glass, then rub the polystyrene rapidly across it... this squeaks like chalk on a blackboard, which seems to be irresistible to the native birds, especially the fantails that dance madly to the rhythm (see T).

On my first visit I sat to rest on one of the benches and tried out this squeaking trick. Quite quickly the birds came to my bench and like St Francis of Assisi birds surrounded me. Whiteheads hung from the branches in front of my face, fantails skittered all around, a curious Tui eyed me from the handrail and a Tomtit foraged between my feet. Saddlebacks even sat next to me on one bench, displaying the sort of curiosity and lack of fear that probably drove them almost to the edge of extinction at the paws of domestic cats and feral ferrets. Out of the bush came Stitchbirds and Bellbirds, which are now almost unknown on most of the mainland.

It's hard to pull yourself away from such a scene – it is so seldom that you can get close to birds... even garden birds back home are less tame than these truly wild charmers. But, if you walk on, you may scatter quails from your path and catch a glimpse of passing seabirds. Indeed, one of the great pleasures of a trip to Tiri is the half-an-hour crossing itself. If there has been a recent storm out at sea, the crossing can be like the most productive pelagic you've ever been on. We had Flesh-footed and Buller's Petrels, terns galore and even a lone Wandering Albatross for company, as well as Hutton's and Sooty Shearwaters with whole flotillas just bobbing about on the waves as we sped by, getting their sea wings back having been blown into the shelter of the Bay.

Usually Little Blue Penguins, which nest on the island occupying incredibly smelly man-made burrows, will follow the boat like tiny torpedoes. You used to be able to pop the lid off these burrows and see the bird inside, if your stomach was strong enough to withstand the assault on your nostrils of old rotten fish and penguin droppings slow-cooking in the heat of the tunnels.

The original driving force behind the regeneration of Tiritiri was the need to save the largest rail in the world, the Takahe, from extinction. If you don't know of this species, then try to imagine a purple gallinule on steroids. It is a really hefty brute of a bird with a beak like a coal chisel and the attitude of a traffic warden. These birds strut about the island establishing territories and seeing off any competitors. They may not mutter 'You can't park 'ere mate', but, just like a traffic warden, they will have you as soon as look at you.

This fearless tendency nearly led to their swan song; running up to hungry colonists, who are a great deal bigger and cleverer than you, is not a good idea. The Takahe that sought to shoo away a human was likely to get bowled over and end up in the pot, even if they are rather tough and fishy tasting, protein was in short supply in the early days of European colonisation.

So, for many years it was thought that they had gone the way of the New Zealand Eagle that starved to death when all the Moas had been eaten by the Maoris, or like the St Stephen's Island Wren, a flightless species, which was extirpated by the St Stephen's Island lighthouse keeper's cat! Then they were re-discovered, like Monty Python's Norwegian Blue Parrot, pining in the fjords! Well almost, they were actually found still hanging on in the high valleys in Fjordland where the mustalids had not managed to become too well established. The remaining Takahe were rounded up and transported to predator-eradicated islands such as Tiri to ensure that their numbers could be built up into a self-sustaining population on several islands before being re-introduced into suitable mainland habitat.

Having found a home for a few territorial Takahe, the guys from Forest & Bird started to add in a few of the other NZ endemics that find it hard to get away from predators... the poor flying Saddlebacks, the confiding North Island Robin and the elusive Stitchbird to name but a few. Moreover, they were soon joined by some of the other natives that find it hard to make it in the modern world, big fat New Zealand Pigeons and Kakariki (Yellow-crowned Parakeet) made it by themselves to this safe haven and happily help spread the native bush with their droppings. More recently Kokako and a native duck have been established there. Uninvited avian visitors are welcomed so long as they carry New Zealand passports; overseas visitors are not even allowed in with a visa.

So Tiri goes from strength to strength – the bush continues to regenerate, the native fauna thrives and even the most emblematic of all New Zealand birds, the kiwi, now has a stronghold.

That first visit by Maggie and me with my parents, sister and niece was a joy never to be forgotten. It lights up in the memory like a beacon of conservation hope. If only all nations, at all times, cared this much for their endangered birds like the hundreds of volunteer 'friends of Tiri' that keep working to ensure the continued success of the preserve.

Time on the island is limited, and after a few hours (unless you are one of the most favoured souls permitted to stay over in the hopes of glimpsing a kiwi, or one of the unpaid student volunteers staying at the bunkhouse) you must assemble to await the tractor to take you back to the jetty and the boat.

While you assemble, the warden's shop and café opens up to part you from your pennies, which, along with the entrance fees, goes a long way to covering all Tiri's conservation costs. Things have probably changed, but when I visited there the shop had very little available, just a few souvenir tea towels, bookmarks, badges and the like. However, they also used to serve a welcoming cup of boiling hot water for you to dangle your teabag in or empty that sachet of drinking chocolate you brought with you and that you must, of course, return to the mainland when it has been emptied.

So there we were, rested from our tramp around the island, breathing its clean air and savouring the sun. We all perched on our open-air, open weave, plastic chairs, waiting for our beverages to cool. At this point, dear reader, you may wonder why there has been no mention of any geese despite the chapter heading, and rightly so as, in fact, Tiritiri Matangi island has no geese at all. There is an isolated muddy pool amidst a patch of swamp where two pairs of native New Zealand Teal idle away there time between attempts to increase their dwindling numbers. But this is as close as you get to any species of geese unless you take the boat back to Auckland and hope for some feral farmyard denizen.

However, and nevertheless, this is where the adumbrated goose entered my life or, rather, that of my sister. For, as we sat perched sipping over hot drinks, the Takahe, who believes that the café is part of his dominion, came noisily upon us. Not content with charging, head down at our knees, he made straight for my sister Jean, ran underneath her chair and rammed his beak for all he was worth through the hole in the seat and into that part of my sister that least often sees the light of day.

The goose was followed by a shriek from Jean as she leapt into the air, leaving the Takahe to look bemused with his head poking up through the plastic seat. We all soon chorused her shrieks as we were liberally showered with her steaming-hot tea.

To this day she is not in the least amused by my continued pleas to submit this happenstance to the *Guinness Book of World Records*. I am convinced that this observation was a world first, given the rarity of the Takahe (there are still only about 300 or so even after all these conservation efforts). Furthermore, it was possibly the last and only Takahe to goose anyone as I gather that those plastic chairs have now been replaced by more solid seating.

…The goose was followed by a shriek from Jean as she leapt into the air leaving the Takahe to look bemused with his head poking up through the plastic seat…

H is for Hummingbird
(Copper-rumped Hummingbird, *Amazilia tobaci*)

Why is it that some species seem iconic and others merely mundane? British birders pay little attention to our humble garden birds, and they inspire less acclaim than 'flashy' birds or some rarer species. But if you take a really close look at a cryptically plumed Dunnock or Wren, you will find that they have a quiet, everyday beauty. Common Starlings are such an every day bird that most birders ignore them, unless they are going through a flock hoping it contains a vagrant Rose-coloured cousin, but their iridescent plumage in the summer sun is seriously stunning. To my mind, on close scrutiny, they rival Macaws or Trogons. Overseas, when you see a Spotless Starling, you can reflect on our resident birds and appreciate that the spotted ones are simply superb.

I am not alone in believing that British birders have good ID skills because many of the birds we see are similar in colour, and variations are quite subtle. To tell American wood warblers apart you need a good memory, but to tell our warblers or woodland tits apart you also need an eye for detail and a good ear for song. However, I cannot deny that, when we take a walk in the woods and come across a Great Spotted Woodpecker, or amble along the canal and see a Kingfisher flash by, our spirits are lifted to the heavens. I suppose they are examples of avian charisma as, no matter what our interest or focus in the birding world, most of us would agree to always feeling thrilled by any owl we see or always being excited by a Hoopoe.

Some birds are iconic not for their plumage, but by association. A screaming Common Swift streaking low to the ground heralds summer like no other, and the call of a Wood Pigeon always evokes a summer evening by fresh water. If we are lucky enough to travel, everything we see will be fresh and new, so both the fascination of novelty and the excitement of discovery come into play, yet still some birds are more equal than others. I'd lay a bet that every birder not brought up in the Americas (and a great many of those who are) will be totally enthralled by the fastest living and smallest of birds of all – the members of the hummingbird family.

Moreover, nearly every hummingbird species, of which there are several hundred, is a living jewel. Even those that at first glance are dull green, or murky brown, will suddenly catch the sun bringing forth a blinding flash of copper, emerald, ruby or violet.

There is also something surreal when you are in the middle of a damp, drizzly wood, in a cold Canadian spring, to catch the movement from the corner of your eye of an insect visiting the early spring flowers, then suddenly to realize that you are looking at a Ruby-throated Hummingbird.

One of the most unforgettable experiences of my life was just a couple of years back when I birded in Panama. We had ridden the open 4x4 for some kilometres along the famous 'Pipeland Road' eventually arriving at a conservation centre set in the forest. The more adventurous and fit can climb a rickety structure up into the canopy to look miles across the forests. Us more rickety birders can sit on a veranda where, if you are lucky, a Little Tinamou may creep by, or you may suddenly realize that a Giant Jacamar has been, all the while, static on a low branch, just feet from your own perch. Most of the time just a few hummers will be flitting to the many feeders along the deck.

When we arrived, I settled down with a welcome (and extremely good) cup of steaming black coffee. The weather suddenly turned, as is often the way in the tropics. The early morning sun had been slowly pushing the temperature up, heading for its afternoon peak, but, as we settled down, the temperature dropped several degrees and then the rain went from a mere misty spray to a torrent in less time than it takes to tell. For the next 40 minutes the rain never lessened, seeming to penetrate the forest like a downpour of needles.

There was an almost immediate and spectacular pay off – every hummingbird that had ever visited the centre before arrived together at the feeders and buzzed about. Maybe as many as 200 individuals, of nine or ten species, sheltered from the rain and sucked sugar from the artificial flowers. White-necked Jacobins bullied diminutive Violet-bellied Hummers, White-vented Plumeteers competed with Long-tailed Hermits and the tiny Little Hermit snuck in almost unnoticed.

I had positioned my chair just before the rain hit, so was right by the veranda rail, two feet from one of the largest feeders, with my arm resting along the rail, almost in touching distance of the feeder. I was still hot and bothered from the sticky heat of the forest, but as the hummers arrived I was suddenly surrounded. Within seconds I was being fanned by the wings of angels, literally feeling the air stirred by their wings as, at times, they were but inches from my face. I am not ashamed to say that this experience almost had me in tears, sheer joy made me grin until my jaw ached! (If you think I am exaggerating then take a look on U-Tube for 'fanned by the wings of angels' and you'll see the footage Maggie managed to film of me.)

I feel that these angels somehow belong south of the Rio Grande. Whenever I have seen hummingbirds in the US, they seem slightly incongruous, and I've never seen more than a handful at any one time. In a cool Texas they seemed less natural than when they are just a couple of hundred miles south into Mexico. There, where hills are covered in tropical vegetation, they start to come into their own. I recall watching a dozen hummers, of three or four species, crowding a bougainvillea opposite the entrance of our lodgings in a wooded area in north-east Mexico. They were the constant in a changing movie, as more than a dozen species of wood warbler moved through the scene on their migration north.

In 2011, I realized a dream by seeing the world's smallest bird in Cuba, the Bee Hummingbird, and, although it is not the only hummer they have, the agricultural landscape seems less than suitable to my eye. In one of the hotels we stayed in, most notable for having West Indian Whistling Duck in the adjacent lagoon, a hummingbird had built a nest in the open foyer above the reception desk. It went unnoticed by 95% of the hotel guests.

My first ever and unforgettable hummingbird encounter was in 1998. Maggie and I took a cheap package to Tobago, as it was the most economical way to bird that island and Trinidad. The flights were in and out of Tobago, but we knew most birds are in Trinidad, so we wanted to get there first for all the South American avifauna before returning to the Caribbean birds in Tobago. We arrived at our Tobago hotel just as dusk was coming down and only had time to marvel at the turquoise Blue-grey Tanagers swooping over the swimming pool before it was too dark to see. Our flight out to Trinidad was due at noon the following day, so I had very little time to bird before getting a cab to the airport for mid-morning.

As always on such trips, I was awake in time to see dawn slowly break and, leaving Maggie to snooze, I slipped out into the very limited hotel grounds. The only greenery was a strip of lawn by the bar, but this was lined with flowering bushes, and, as I arrived, I saw my second trip 'lifer' sitting up in the bush – a wonderfully zebra-striped Barred Antshrike – terrific, my overseas birding smile started to creep across my face.

I soon realized that I was not alone; further along the bush was a stocky, white-haired man gripping a complex camera and trying to photograph something that was clearly on the move. I joined him to see the sudden red-orange flash of a Copper-rumped Hummingbird. The photographer must have heard my sharp intake of breath at this flash of brilliance, as he chanced a comment: 'Neat, hey?', thus revealing his origins as a Canadian. I explained that this was my very first hummingbird. He told me that he was a life-long birder and was particularly entranced by the beauty of tanagers. We chatted a little before I took my leave, explaining that we had to breakfast before transferring to Trinidad. His parting shot was that he hoped to see me there, as he and his wife were moving on too in a few days.

Three or four days later we had tucked dozens of lifers under our belts and were ensconced on the veranda of the Asa Wright Nature Centre. This wonderful Lodge overlooks a valley stretching 20 kilometres down to the town. There tiny areas of primary forest have been joined up by secondary growth, since coffee plantations were abandoned and have been reclaimed by nature over a number of decades.

Asa Wright is one of those places I see in my mind's eye when I speculate on what an afterlife *ought* to be like. For me the scenario is obvious; I want somewhere that perfectly combines the pastimes I most enjoy: birding, lazing about, eating and sipping the occasional libation. Asa Wright fits the bill. Caribbean food is served in copious quantities, from substantial breakfasts to sumptuous dinners via a number of snacking opportunities, such as a colonial style afternoon tea. Can there be anything more civilized than watching birds, with a canapé pastry in the shape of a swan in one hand and a spicy rum punch in the other? There, in front of you, stretches the regenerating bush, Amazon Parrots flying by with Turkey Vultures soaring above, a Wattled Bellbird calling from a Cecropia tree, where a Woodcreeper inches along a branch. As you lean over the railing, you can watch a parade of avian delights visiting the feed table, which is piled high with overripe fruit.

A Chestnut Woodpecker walks about taking his pick of the best, while dislodging fruit crumbs that are snatched up by a shy black and white Great Antshrike that spots the morsels with its beady red eye. A flurry of tanagers muscle in, with dull Palm Tanagers shoulder to shoulder with bright Silver-beaked Tanagers. Nipping in and out are Trinidad Euphonias and brilliant Purple Honeycreepers with their green mates. What the birds don't eat falls to the floor to be vacuumed up by jittery Agoutis or slow moving Green Iguanas.

Perched above the rail are half a dozen hummingbird feeders which are emptied by the birds almost as quickly as they are filled, and around about the lodge there are bottlebrush bushes and bougainvillea flowers to be supped from, when the Honey Creepers are hogging the feeders.

So there I was, that fourth day in heaven, pontificating to some new arrivals and anyone else who would listen. I was delving into the bottomless depths of my incredibly extensive experience of the local hummingbirds. One moment I was pointing out the difference between a Black-throated Mango and a Long-billed Starthroat, the next minute I extolled the virtues of the brightly coloured Blue-tailed Emerald. Then I was trying to get these novices to see a Tufted Coquette, which kept disappearing into the foliage of the bottlebrush bush.

Out of nowhere a firm hand descended on my shoulder. 'Will you listen to this guy,' intoned a deep Canadian voice, 'three days ago he hadn't even seen a hummingbird, and now he's a bloody expert!' Needless to say 'Mo' and I have been firm friends ever since and have even managed to bird together a couple of times on our visits to Texas and Canada and when he visited the UK.

'Will you listen to this guy', intoned a deep Canadian voice, 'Three days ago he hadn't even seen a hummingbird, and now he's a bloody expert!'

I is for Indian Lark
(Indian Bush Lark, *Mirafra erythroptera*)

Bharatpur Bird Sanctuary (part of the Keoladeo Ghana National Park) is in the state of Rajasthan in India. It is one of those myriad of places across the world that local tourist authorities invariably label 'a birders' paradise'. However, unlike many an undeserving spot, it really is an iconic destination. When the rains have filled its lakes, marshes and ditches, and soaked every bush and blade of grass, it is truly wondrous – like France's Camargue, Brazil's Pantanal or Florida's Everglades, it is a vast wetland – food-filled and bird bountiful.

Naturally when Maggie and I, and our mixed party of disabled and able-bodied birders visited, it was bone dry – save for the ground water deliberately pumped up to sustain the dwindling fauna. Even so, it takes its rightful place as one of the top birding hot spots I've ever been to and not just because of the superb birdlife.

We stayed close to the park in a hotel that had been created by converting an old palace. This is the one and only time in my life when my hotel room came replete with its own indoor fountain! The room was the very epitome of 'shabby chic'. The distempered walls scattered peeling paint onto the hand-made rugs and over the marble-topped tables. Dust had settled on the carved headboard and the wall hangings had faded from constant exposure to India's unforgiving sun. The hotel gave us many memorable moments. They included the high point of savouring the very best Tempura I've ever eaten, and the low point of sitting through the most incomprehensible puppet show I've not managed to avoid. Swallows swooping into their nests on the high palace, parapets accompanied our early morning breakfast in the open quadrangle within the palace, and mornings were not heralded by crowing cockerels but rather by the piercing calls of wild peacocks.

Early the next morning we left for the park, pausing only briefly to observe a smelly pool beloved of the local Pygmy Cormorants and Waterhens. To enter the reserve, a tour group is required to have an 'official' guide assigned and everyone must go into the park aboard a rickshaw – the only exceptions being the officials and, in our case, wheelchair users who get instead to be pushed the whole way.

Being horizontally challenged (alright, fat) and having a partner who has also left her svelte days behind, I felt some trepidation. I did not think it fair that either my bulk, or even the lesser burden of my beloved, should have to be hauled by another human being... particularly, in my case, a rather small chap clearly in his sixth decade. I would not want to deprive him of his livelihood, but it felt like a real imposition to be such a burden.

It is embarrassing for most British people to be waited upon or to have some other personal service undertaken by another. This probably explains why British waiters, porters and associated trades have a reputation for rudeness and haughtiness. Presumably, they too feel that it's way out of order that any person should be servile to any other just to earn a crust. Shoeshine boys (of any age) may still be extant in some climes but not in Blighty! Just like tipping, or responding to cheek kissing, we Brits just don't handle such situations well.

However, India is, as in so many other ways, a total exception. As you travel its roads you will see every human function and service on display. Ordinary people go about their ablutions 'al fresco' and pay others to shave their faces, wash their clothes or even clean out their earwax! The peoples of India have the necessary ability to ignore the open display of much that we in the west keep private. It is as normal for them to live life without walls, as it is to show their open curiosity at the bizarre antics of us foreigners. For example, when, on another trip, our taxi hit the back of another vehicle, which was trying to avoid a cow that was asleep in the middle of the road on a blind bend, the whole village came to peer at us. Faces pressed against the taxi windows, asking if we needed an ambulance or treatment for whiplash, or just to grin and stare. Within minutes the whole village had polarized into camps as to who was at fault. On the other hand, during this trip, when we saw a cow cartwheel through the air after being hit full on by an unfenced freight train, no one batted an eye. We stared open-mouthed, half in shock, but the people went about their daily business as if this was an every day sight. Who knows? Perhaps it was. Nevertheless, a rickshaw was not optional; we had either to comply or dip out on a visit to this unique wetland area, and that was just not an option. Our party was assigned a rather dapper guide through the usual noisy and participatory process by which everything seems to happen in India. Then we were free to set off in search of birds.

The pace was slow in order that even the least observant amongst us would not miss out on anything, so it took a whole morning to reach the turning point of the tour. All the time along the route the official guide pointed out birds, or where those birds should have been, but often were not. It became clear that this guide was no naturalist, and it occurred to us that he must be someone's favourite nephew or cousin, appointed to a plum post through graft rather than his expertise. Obviously, over time in the job, he had picked up a thing or two, but occasionally he made an error in ID so obvious that even our novice birders noticed. However, he never, ever, got one past our rickshaw wallah.

Whenever the guide made a dodgy ID, our chap would do the subtlest of head-wiggles that one only sees in the sub-continent. Of course, this can mean agreement, a question or just a bodily 'OK' but, very clearly, in his case it was dissent. As the guide had got a bit ahead of us, we did not always catch what he said, but we could tell when to look in the direction he indicated by glancing at our rickshaw man. If his head didn't wobble we paid attention to the guide, if his head shimmied we looked elsewhere.

The classic case was when the guide assured us all that Stone Curlews used to be seen along the road but had all left a few weeks ago… this prompted a positive paroxysm of neck and head movement. Our man pulled the rickshaw around, took us 20 yards back down the road and pointed between the bushes to three birds. They stood stock-still, large, yellow eyes wide-open, looking back at us in a most Thick-kneed way!

We trusted the man who had pulled his rickshaw along the same route for 20 years over the official with his crisp new uniform. Mr Singh, encouraged by our acclamation, began to point the birds out to us in a loud stage whisper so as not to be too obviously undermining his 'superior'. We clocked up some real goodies missed by those ahead with, for me, the top bird being a beautifully cryptic Brown-capped Pigmy Woodpecker. Many others followed, culminating in the excitement of seeing an owl roosting in a hollow tree.

Mr Singh took a deserved rest with the other rickshaw wallahs as we ate our packed lunch and found shelter from the midday sun… only interrupted by being called together by our tour guide and walked to a spot where a large Indian Python lay sunning itself, coiled in the dust.

Having been fed and watered, one of our number asked if one of our tour guides would take him to see a bird that he had missed. He was happy to go on birding in the heat of the day and making the chap guide him during his meal break. While he was away the top bird of the day briefly emerged from the scrub close to the group. Our tour operator managed to tick a lifer for himself and share his find with the group. The cryptic and generally crepuscular Smokey Warbler made it on to everyone's list except our absent friends... so justice was served.

When the heat peak passed, we were taken to view a plain from the raised bund where we had distant and heat haze-distorted views of Indian Courser. A top sighting that rivalled our earlier views of Sociable Plover. The latter bird had caused a real stir. The able-bodied raced across a field to view the bird, which necessitated scrambling through a hedge as the bird was on the far side. The rest of us limped, hobbled or wheeled as fast as we could so as not to dip out... everyone made it, some surprising quickly! It's amazing what the need to tick a 'lifer' will bring out of even the most infirm of birders. When confronted with the prospect of dipping out, some are like mothers imbued with superhuman strength for just long enough to lift a vehicle away from their injured child. They say you must suffer for your art; well, a sleepless night in pain brought on by overdoing things is often well worth it to those of us with the birding obsession.

Close to our picnic spot was a pool where groundwater was being pumped and was as thick with birds as it is possible to be. Perhaps 200 Citrine Wagtails adorned bare branches, clothing them as if with summer leaves or bobbed and hopped around the pool fringes finding flies to chase. Ruddy Shelduck positively assaulted one's retinas with their burnt orange hues. Herons and storks, Greenshank and sandpipers, finches and doves crowded the bushes, pond margins and exposed mud. Best of all, sitting in the shallows as if enthroned, was the most magnificent Steppe Eagle allowing our naked eyes to see its crucial ID feature, the gape that characteristically extends further back than its eye.

Afterwards we slowly retraced our rickshaw path back toward the park entrance. As the light faded, we were serenaded by the haunting calls of Golden Jackals. At first they were quite distant, then the calls got louder until we realized that they ran in a pack alongside our path just out of sight of the rickshaws… paradise indeed – although Brian reported afterwards that maybe they were just a tad too close to his exposed wheelchair for comfort, and he had speculated as to whether he could be hauled into the relative safety of a rickshaw. As he pedalled slowly through the gloom, our rickshaw man pointed out a firefly or two to remind Maggie of the story he had told her earlier. When we had sat relaxing at lunchtime Mr Singh had pointed out some weavers' nests to Maggie. They hung from thorn bushes and danced in the light breeze.

'The males', he explained to her, 'do all the work of building the nests, then they must compete for the females by showing off their handiwork. The males with the best nests get the girls. But,' as he also pointed out, 'the nests are perfect spheres with an entrance tunnel, so it is very dark inside the nests and hard for the females to see.' 'How do you think the females can judge which is best?' he asked, and Maggie hazarded a guess. Was it the feel on the soft lining, or perhaps the female could see how well the nest was woven from the outside?

Mr Singh wobbled his head gleefully before telling her. 'The male weaver bird collects fireflies and pops them inside the nest so that the females can see that his work is the finest!' Maggie was open-mouthed with incredulity. 'Do they really?' she asked in amazement. Mr Singh's head wobbled all the more as his grin broadened. 'Of course not!' he roared before bursting into uncontrollable laughter, so infectious that even an embarrassed Maggie joined in.

'The male weaver bird collects fireflies and pops them inside the nest so that the females can see that his work is the finest!'

J is for Jacamar
(Rufous-tailed Jacamar, *Galbula ruficauda*)

In 1999, Maggie and I visited my folks in New Zealand and decided that en route we would spend a few days in Thailand birding in the famous Khao Yao National Park. This was to be our first overseas birding trip where we had made all our own arrangements to a country where most people do not speak English. This is often the cheapest way to get to see the birds but is by no means the easiest; what's more, it is seldom the most productive – it certainly pays to be with someone who knows what birds are where.

So we arrived in Bangkok on a typically close and sweaty evening, tired out from many hours in 'steerage' and anxious to get to our hotel and bed before we dropped. We knew that it was quite a distance to the hotel that we had booked because of its proximity to the park, so we had arranged to be met at the airport and transferred. We reclaimed our bags and dragged them through customs and, not seeing anyone with our name on a placard, struggled out onto the street. Walking out into that heat was like walking into a solid wall. There was a second wall to bring us up short, the impervious barrier of the traffic noise. Bangkok is a mega city with around 20 million inhabitants, and they all seemed to be going to, past or from the airport. Discomforted by the heat and disoriented by the noise, we struggled down a taxi ramp where tour busses, cabs and limousines all jostled for places. Our hopes for a smooth transfer rose as we saw that some drivers were paging their passengers. However, others were just touting for business and, to my irritation, we were soon approached too. A smiling Thai tugged at my sleeve…'Tourist?' he asked. I nodded assent, but told him we did not need his services because the company that had made our arrangements would be meeting us. 'Tourist?' he asked again… I shook my head and waved him away. 'Tourist?' He said yet again, more insistently, with yet another smile. They say that there are thirteen ways to smile in Thailand, and we had already seen two, but I didn't understand either. Angrily I shook his hand from my sleeve and gathering up our bags, and, taking Maggie's arm, I steered us away from this persistent tout.

Tiredness and heat was getting to Maggie too, and she was beginning to get exasperated with me, insisting that I look up the name of the company that was meeting us… soon I was spilling papers and other bits and pieces from my hand luggage onto the paving. I eventually waved some papers in triumph and together we looked for the company name… Thailand Adventures.

We began to ask people if they were the rep we were looking for. Most of them just shook their heads, understanding not one word of what we were saying. Although I made sure I raised my voice and talked slowly in the time-honoured manner of an Englishman abroad, they were impervious to reason or just too obdurate to help. Watching us accosting all and sundry soon attracted back the taxi tout; he elbowed his way through the gathering throng to hassle us once more. 'Tourist!' he insisted even louder than before, and I shook my head turning away to try and avoid his gaze, but he snatched the paper from my hand before I could stop him. He smoothed the crumpled sheets out on his thigh and then held it aloft, shaking it literally under my nose. He pointed at the line of print under the main header and shouted 'Tourist! Tourist!' all the while brandishing my papers or holding them steady so that I could see... and there it was, under the header of 'Thailand Adventures', the second line held the legend, '...A division of TOUR EAST'!

I looked at my feet as the blood flushed my cheeks a deep red. Then the patient and persistent Thai took our bags from us, and we sheepishly followed him to the waiting vehicle. He ushered us into the car, wearing an even more different smile, and began to drive away at a snail's pace through the heavy traffic. Our spirits slumped further as we realised that it was going to be a long haul to our hotel.

It was a strange journey there... we watched the passing city with its lily-choked canals and millions of mopeds all with horns blaring. As the buildings thinned at the outskirts of the city, the countryside seemed to us to be rich and cultivated. Every crossroads boasted a temple or shrine, although it became harder and harder to see them in the gathering gloom.

The longer the journey went on, the more a broken pipe from the cab's air-conditioning dripped water on us, dampening our clothes to match our spirits. We tried to engage the driver in conversation, but our lack of Thai language, combined with his lack of English, meant we only had smiles and gestures to communicate through. Even this was made difficult, as he had to attend to driving the crowded thoroughfares where all road rules seemed to be optional. Two hours had dragged by and we were tired beyond feeling when the driver stopped to re-fuel. Somehow we managed to act out the question 'how much longer would it take', and he looked despondent then pointed to his watch and carefully did ten revolutions of the dial with his finger. How could we have been so wrong? Surely it couldn't take another ten hours? Ten minutes later we turned into the driveway of our hotel. We were greeted by a veritable parade of staff lined up to receive us with bows, flower necklaces and nods and smiles. We signed the register and were then shown to our room.

I asked at the desk if they had heard from the guide that we had engaged to show us the park early the next morning, and were told 'no' by the young lady at reception. She appeared to be the only one who spoke any English but revealed that she was going on leave the next day. She also explained to us that we were the only guests in the entire hotel.

Even though we had not eaten for many hours, we decided to go to bed after ringing room service to order a take-away breakfast for the next day. Looking down the menu I asked if I could have a tuna sandwich and ordered a bacon one for Maggie. Half an hour later 'breakfast' arrived. I took it in and by a gestures and mime managed to order it all over again for the next day!

Up early the next morning, we dressed in the dark and got our optics and ourselves to reception and were met by the same driver as the day before. We unravelled our breakfast parcels to find the same soggy toasted sandwiches and grey fries as we had had the night before... this seemed the only thing available from room service on each occasion we called upon them over several days. Indeed I was forced to use room service for most of my stay as the only non-meat meal that the restaurant served was as foul tasting as it was beautiful. A whole fish, replete with carrots carved into roses and other veg chiselled into straws amidst a thin sauce, looked the prettiest of pictures. However, it seemed to me on tasting that the fish had been left in the sun for a week and then served in gravy made with cough medicine. I am sure this was the finest of foods and would be adored by others, but it was not at all to my taste.

The drive from our hotel just outside of the park, into its very middle where there is a visitor centre, took an hour, but the journey started well when a Long-tailed Nightjar flew in front of us having taken off from the warmth of the road. As the sun gradually rose, we saw that there was elephant dung around every bend. Clearly there was either a very sizeable herd of elephants inhabiting the park or a lesser number of extremely incontinent ones.

We arrived at the Centre well before it opened to the public and then hung around waiting for our guide to meet us. The very kind driver stayed with us, even though he clearly had other things to do. There followed an hour of increasing frustration, broken only by a stunning Scarlet Minivet displaying in the treetops and the arrival of some other visitors and park staff. We eventually found someone to ask about the guide, to be told that he actually lived in the park in some dwellings behind the centre. Poking about, we managed to locate our guide snoring in his cabin. When we roused him it was clear that he had not managed to entirely sleep off the alcoholic over-indulgence of the night before and was still unsteady on his feet. He did understand a little English and told us he would be with us in two minutes. Half an hour later he turned up at the front of the centre, still dishevelled and bleary eyed, and beckoned us to follow him into the forest.

We dogged his steps over a swinging bridge, across a river and into the forest. Here he showed us Tiger pug marks (which were small enough to have been his pet tabby), then began to point out the birds, which he flushed in such as way that they immediately bolted into the canopy. It only took a few minutes to realize that he was not only late and drunk, but also totally ignorant about the birds. We told him his services were not required and retraced our steps to the Park Centre. Here we found that our driver was still hanging about. He explained, through one of the English-speaking park staff, that he had rung the hotel and was not needed so could accompany us if we wished. Frankly, he saved the day for us, and we went on to find some great birds for ourselves and get a taster of what Thailand has to offer.

By now you are probably thinking that none of this has anything to do with Jacamars and, anyway, aren't they birds from an entirely different continent? Well spotted, dear reader… in truth the theme of this piece is not so much to do with any particular bird but more about the failure to communicate through a language barrier. Often this is due to one's own stupidity as the 'Tour East' incident aptly demonstrates, but sometimes it's all about the difficulty that English in general, and bird names in particular, can pose to those not used to speaking it.

The bird in the title was shown to us in Trinidad. Our driver had told us that he knew a place where some birds nested in holes in a bank on the side of the road. Intrigued we asked what they were called, to which he replied 'Jack Hammers'! Of course, when he finally got us to the nest site we had excellent views of Jacamars. To be fair, although the driver was a native English speaker, he was not a birder and was trying to help us out, having driven us to wherever we asked him to, as we followed old trip reports in search of close encounters of the avian kind.

Same place, different driver, had us trying to follow his pointed finger into a bush to see the Salt Eater that he assured us was there. In fact, we were very specifically in pursuit of the Great Salt Eater Bird that he had intrigued us with. This was no 'civilian' but a professional bird guide taking us to see a bird that we could find nowhere in our field-guide. Having, at last, managed to get decent views of the bird, we were able to leaf confidently through the book until we found the very same as an excellent illustration – a Grey Saltator.

The very pinnacle of this type of misunderstanding was in India when we were birding in and around Corbett National Park, guided by one of the finest bird guides we've had the good fortune to meet up with. This was a trip we had put together for the 'disabled birders association' (now called 'Birding For All') with the help of Asian Adventures run by a good friend of ours – Mohit Argawaal. His top guide is father to another of the company's up and coming guides. The son has perfect English, but the less well-educated father is streets ahead as a bird finder.

Like many Indian people we have birded with, Ratan has a great sense of humour combined with a pride in his work – he would brave hellfire to get the customer a lifer. He has a terrific ear too, so would find as many target birds by recognizing distant calls and honing in on them, as well as spotting birds from the merest flutter of a distant frond. However, there were also times when it was hard to get exactly what he was saying – it took me a while to be sure what he was referring to with quite a lot of birds, but two in particular took a lot of translation. The first was the Wet-Biscuit Booboo… this was a bird that seemed to be calling everywhere we went, but it was only when it was firmly framed in my binoculars that I was sure I had the right name – Red-whiskered Bulbul.

The other intrigue was a denizen of the garden of the Lodge we were staying just on the park boundary. I had heard Ratan refer to the Bird-eating Flycatcher a number of times when we were hunting down Chestnut-tailed Starlings. I heard the name again when we had wonderful views of a Velvet Nuthatch and a Tickell's Blue Flycatcher. Shortly afterwards another bird flew into a bush right beside the veranda where we were idly birding as we sipped cold beer. It turned out to be the very bird in question – a beautiful Verditer Flycatcher.

Our driver had told us that he knew a place where some birds nested in holes in a bank on the side of the road. Intrigued we asked what they were called, to which he replied 'Jack Hammers'! Of course, when he finally got us to the nest site we had excellent views of Jacamars.

K is for Kalij Pheasant
(Kalij Pheasant, *Lophura leucomelanos*)

The common pheasant is a familiar site all over the world having been widely introduced to the Americas, New Zealand and across Europe. It is native to parts of Asia and the Middle East, and a number of related species can be found in the Indian sub-continent and much of Indo-China. Until my first trip to Northern India I had only ever seen the one species.

At the start of our trip we had been chasing another familiar fowl – Red Jungle Fowl, the ancestor of domestic chickens. We had finally managed a brief glimpse in Corbett National Park – lucky for me this particular individual ran towards and passed our vehicle as, until then, only the people in the jeep at the front had connected with these superb birds. Our group had a number of guides and drivers in order to make sure there were always sufficient able-bodied people around to help the disabled birders who made up half the group. One guide had an edge over the others in his bird spotting skills, so anyone who could made sure they joined his vehicle, which also tended to be at the front. (Thereby hangs an entirely different tale the moral of which is, if you have to bird in convoy make sure the lead vehicles swap around!) The drivers were all good-natured youngsters, but most were not really interested in birding. Being young men of a certain age meant their interests were sport and girls (not necessarily in that order) or maybe a mixture of the two. Inevitably this also meant that they were in constant competition with each other, and this necessitated a great deal of posing. Indian poseurs tend to strike poses only otherwise seen in Bollywood movies, which, to my mind, are not unlike a great deal of the behaviour exhibited in male birds trying to attract mates – lots of neck stretching, shoulder shrugging and lofty, disdainful looks.

We had travelled to the park from Delhi in a large bus driven by a more mature driver who was used to the impossible road conditions in India. If you have never been to India, it is hard to describe the extent of the terror one can feel driving along their roads! An Indian friend says he will not drive in the UK because there are so many confusing rules. In India there seem to be no rules at all to confuse anyone, just a lot of grim determination, machismo and use of the horn. They say that any vehicle is roadworthy unless the horn doesn't work and driving seems to be a mixture of using the horn repeatedly and often, macho brinkmanship and oriental fatalism (see Y).

To illustrate the way things are, a perfect example occurred on day one. We drove down a duel carriageway in the heart of Delhi on our way to birdwatch at the Barrage – an area of farmland where the river sometimes floods, causing the area to be fringed with pools, mud and reedy swamp, and so it is rich in birds. Our tour operator told us we were nearing our destination when the vehicle made an unexpected U-turn through a gap in the central reservation and then drove a couple of hundred yards against the traffic flow before turning off down a dirt track. No one said anything, the Indian members of the party were totally un-phased, but the Brits had drawn in their breath so deep that they couldn't speak let alone cry out in alarm! It was as if we were at the bow of an ice-breaker as vehicles turned aside and drove around us at the last possible moment.

On the long journey to Corbett we had become used to driving down a two-track road with five lanes of traffic coming right at you. We were also used to seeing every possible type of land vehicle there is. On any Indian road you can encounter camels, elephants and carts powered by old water pumps steered with a tiller, as well as every motorised vehicle from the latest sports cars to air-conditioned super coaches. We were also used to seeing many vehicles rusting on their sides in ditches along the route. It was difficult not to begin to absorb some of the fatalism, but it was never quite sufficient to overcome the abject terror just before the moment the five lanes of traffic parted allowing your survival. Every such moment was greeted with the sudden release of held breath or the crescendo in both volume and pitch of an elongated expletive. My solution was to keep watching everything going on until we built up speed on a 'better' road, then it was time to close the eyes rather than suffer the frequent and rapid anxiety attacks.

The day we transferred from Corbett to the town of Nainital a few thousand feet up in the Himalayas was a mixture of elation (wonderful views) and terror (horrifying drops). On the flat the roads seem to spread out to allow the passage of traffic, albeit sometimes confined by evil smelling ditches. These ditches are often open sewers, yet they are beloved of birds, with the ordure often being picked over by Pied Stilts. However, there was no such leeway as the roads began to wind up the foothills of the Himalayas. Occasionally, when there were no precipitous drops the road was wide enough to comfortably accommodate a decent sized truck coming one way and a broad-bellied coach going the other. But, for the most part, and always when there were sheer drops of a hundred feet or more, the roads were narrow, barely seeming able to allow all four wheels of a coach to straddle tarmac. If a truck trundled around a bend, it had to slow in order to edge by, and one could see the fine detail of each line and curlicue of their exquisite painted decoration. I cannot recall at what stage we moved from the coach into several 'Gypsies' (Jeep-like open vehicles). Obviously, this was because the coach needed to go a slower wider route and we went the faster, narrower way to our next hotel a mile higher as the vulture soars. I found that it was much harder to close my eyes and trust in karma… because we were now open to the elements. As the road wound ever upwards, one would go from sunlight to shadow at every turn. Out of the shade the sun was still hot and high in the sky, around each bend the shadow of the hills kept the sun away and snow lay in the hollows. I imagine that, were a pig not dead and was spit-roasted, it would feel just like I felt. The pig, like us, would fear for its life on the scary roads and, like us, would burn and freeze on each revolution of the spit.

I was not alone in having knuckles the colour of the snow, frigidly clutching the sides of my seat as we diced with death defying drops each time we emerged into the sun. The road, the drops, the heat and cold would have been sufficient for this coward to endure, however, our young drivers conspired to add further fear to my quaking soul. They were posing to each other using their rear-view mirrors to communicate. Each half turned in the driver's seat using just one hand on the steering wheel as we rocked and rolled along the road. I was able to hide my fear from my companions by shivering with cold; one shiver looking very like another, yet I found my ire rising with the altitude. It was no concern of mine if the lads were leaving their fate to a higher power, but I was not disposed to trust in their, or anyone else's, deities. Later, they found their pride had to be swallowed when we met up with the bus and their boss who tore them back down to embarrassed boys. The boss was a terrific bloke, who treats his staff like family, even to the extent of paying for extra education. He is egalitarian always taking his turn at tiresome tasks or any privation. In return he expects and gets the utmost respect. To be dressed down by him cannot be shrugged off because he is scrupulously fair.

Despite my graven timidity I did what every birder does when on such a trip. I kept my eyes out for birds – during the ride I spotted a bird scuttling away from the road down the steep slope and into the trees – a sparkling black and white Kalij Pheasant – a lifer!

Nainital is a fantastic place; the town looks as if it was first built thousands of years ago and that each generation has added a bit here and a bit there. Houses up to five or six stories sit on ancient foundations, and each floor can have a different style. The town crowds around an alpine lake and then creeps up the sides of the surrounding steep hillsides. At the end of the valley there are sheer drops to the Indian plain a mile below. Here we re-joined the coach and sat for a while waiting for one of the 'Gypsies' to re-join us. Glancing out of the window I ticked another lifer as a Bar-tailed Tree-creeper crept up the side of a town tree.

On the move again the coach wound up and around the town making for our hotel, several times having to back up and re-route when the road was too steep or the corners too narrow for the bus to manoeuvre around. Finally, we arrived at the hotel as evening was giving way to night, and the group assembled, shivering in the foyer as the temperature sank as quickly as the sun.

Half of the building, including the dining room, was partitioned off, alerting us that the hotel was being renovated. There was nowhere to eat, but we gave simple food orders (we went for boiled eggs) to the receptionist who promised they would be delivered to our rooms along with our luggage. The rooms were freezing as the hotel boiler had been removed awaiting replacement. Staff rallied round with heaters that barely warmed the immediate few inches in front of them. Maggie kept her coat on, then removed her shoes and climbed into bed, tucking the bedclothes around her and sitting up to await the evening 'breakfast', looking for all the world like a WW2 Russian refugee. An age latter the eggs arrived hidden under cosies; the epitome of Britishness of several generations ago.

I cannot recall where or how we breakfasted the next day, but I do recall walking around the back of the hotel and into its courtyard... this was a small square of lawn that was more earth than grass surrounding a very sad tree... perhaps a birch that had just two upright leafless limbs. Nevertheless, it held an amazing three lifers for me, all types of tit! I walked around the front of the building to join the coach, and there under a bush was yet another (sub-species) lifer – Orange-flanked Bush-robin.

We spent the day in the area seeing avifauna that is completely different from much of the subcontinent. There were some excellent birds, including close views of the enormous Lammergeyer. One small incident stands out that has nothing to do with birding and everything to do with India. Maggie and other members of the party were experiencing, thankfully mild, tummy upsets often called, and with reason, Delhi Belly. We were on the outskirts of a small village when the cramps struck, and we asked our tour operator if there was any local facility we could use and he made enquiries for us. There was a village toilet, which Maggie made for. The detail is not something one would wish to share, but the toilet, although acceptable in cleanliness and design, had one disconcerting feature... the door was made from fence staves and rotten boards so that the gaps were just the right size for the village children to crowd around and peer through at the strange foreigner in their midst. The drug of choice for travelling birders – Imodium – safely prevented any more such moments for Maggie.

As so often with birding trips, the high moments far outweigh the low, and we all enjoyed the cool woods and streams, and saw some great birds during the two days there, perhaps the top bird being the Spotted Forktail. However, the bird that I remember best was neither particularly uncommon nor overwhelmingly attractive.

Our tour operator decided that our second day should start further up in the hills at around 7000 feet amid the pine forest. This was not to see particular birds so much as to avoid Holi – the festival where powdered paint is thrown at everyone. He told us that this tended to peter out around lunchtime, because those most enthusiastically pelting people with paint would have succumbed to a liberal consumption of alcohol and would be sleeping it off.

We started the day standing around an open fire warming ourselves with occasional forays in search of birds. The one that fascinated me was the Grey Tit. This looks exactly like the European Great Tit, yet it is a separate species. Indeed, there is a local race of Great Tit that looks nothing like the one at home as it is rather washed out and grey. If ever there was proof that birding ID is strictly for the nerds then this is it! At lunchtime we descended to another site where there was a cabin, used to prepare a very tasty lunch for us while we birded the grounds, lapping up Rufus-chinned Laughingthrush and a plethora of Hume's Warblers. There were a few other birders there, and I was chatting with a couple of lads from England who mentioned having used Fatbirder when planning their trip and had been told that the person behind it was on a trip here too. At this point, an Indian birder who was within earshot ran over and threw his arms around me! He then told me that we had been corresponding for many years! This is another of the great things about our hobby, the fellowship of fellow birders is as worldwide as the internet.

'*They were posing to each other using their rear-view mirrors to communicate. Each half turned in the driver's seat using just one hand on the steering wheel as we rocked and rolled along the road. I was able to hide my fear from my companions by shivering with cold; one shiver looking very like another...*'

L is for Lovebirds
(Fischer's Lovebird, *Agapornis personata fischeri*)

I have seen lovebirds in the wild, just once – in Kenya, well away from where the books say they range. Fortunately, I was not alone; eight other people saw them too, so this was no illusion. A pair of Fischer's Lovebirds was sitting on a branch and they were very definitely smooching.

I love birds, but many of the most memorable moments while on birding trips are not bird sightings but of non-avian life that I have heard. Maybe it is because I am, primarily, visually oriented that memories are much more often evoked by smell or sound – my hearing having deteriorated over the years, but I still love music and birdsong. Even when my hearing was perfect, I was terrible at recognising bird calls. I can commit to memory the nuances of some very cryptic plumages, but even simple songs seem to seep out of my brain after a matter of hours. A very few stay put and even those I have no confidence in. If I hear a Blackbird singing in the garden I recognise it, but put its song alongside that of a Song Thrush and I'll begin to worry that I have it wrong. Throw in a Robin, Blackcap and Garden Warbler and I just give up. Nevertheless, some other sounds can take me instantly back in time and space, and I can visualise every blade of grass or leaf on the trees at that time and that place. A few sounds are emotionally neutral, but most carry the memory of a particular moment's feelings, just as much as they do space and time.

Many cultures have demons or spirits that are the 'terror of the air', making spine-chilling noises in the night. In New Zealand, the Maoris feared and respected the calls of the once much more widespread and abundant Takahe and thought it best left alone as they believed it to be a harbinger of death. In Ireland banshees terrify one in the night with their blood-curdling screams. I have no idea what the equivalent myth is in Kenya, but I do know that the noises made at night by Tree Hyrax are the scariest natural noises I've ever heard. When we stayed at Narro Morro River Lodge near Mount Kenya and were walking back to our cabin from the dining room, tree hyraxes decided to suddenly scream and put the fear of God into us! Now there *is* a sound I would instantly recognise.

When it rained heavily one afternoon in Panama, we went back to our room and catch up with some of the sleep lost to early rising to trundle down the 'Pipeline Road'. But our slumber was washed away by the sudden close clamouring of Howler Monkeys that decided to have a ruck right outside our window. Not as scary as the sound of the Tree Hyrax, but it's still a shock when you are slipping into the arms of Morpheus and they bellow in your ear.

Nighttime or early morning seem to be favoured for focusing sound, whether it causes night terrors or becomes a lasting memory of a special moment.

On our way back to our hotel in Naivasha National Park in Kenya having been owling, every puddle seem to be an echo chamber for a variety of frog species. Listening to their bubble and squeak and resonating croaks was better than a human orchestra. We stopped our vehicle and wound down the windows just to wallow in the sounds from the mud-wallowing frogs.

Haunting tends to be used as a pejorative term, but my silent hours are often pleasantly haunted by the sounds that speak of early mornings waking in a foreign land ready to see new birds. The distant, echoing call of Peacocks in India is brought back and multiplied every time the call is heard in the background of a country estate during a TV programme. The call can instantly transport you from an English summer afternoon to the cool of an Indian early morning where the birds seem to take turns to wake and join the wild symphony.

Undoubtedly, the most evocative sound of all and the one that almost always brings wistful tears to my eyes is that of Gibbons calling in the rainforests of Asia. I have twice walked along a jungle path as the dawn mists were still hanging in the hollows and heard their wonderfully mournful calls echoing across a forest clearing. Once in Malaya where the condensing mist was dripping form the trees and hardly a bird called, suddenly the conversation between these delightful primates began. But my best memory was walking along a road in Thailand many years ago as the morning light broke through the canopy and the sun began to dry out the mist. Before the day truly took hold, the White-handed Gibbons called back and forth across a vast cleared area, and we could see them languidly lolling, their tails hanging like vines from big tree boughs. I've seen people well up when talking about swimming with dolphins, but sharing dawn with gibbons does it for me.

Very few smells evoke birding places, perhaps because nature's smells tend to be more subtle than the stench of cities. Some cities definitely have their own aroma, like Singapore that smells of cloves, as clove cigarettes are still popular there. Urban Thailand always smells of barbeques, as many vendors of street food use charcoal to heat their offerings. Many Indian villages smell of the sweet smoke given off by dried cowpat fires. Leningrad underground systems smells of stale, vodka-laden breath. Nevertheless, there are a few smells that do transport me to places I have birded. Eucalyptus oil takes me back to one particular day driving from the coast of Queensland up to

Atherton Tablelands. On a long winding road through open rocky-floored forest we stopped as I heard a strange loud hissing that I thought might be air leaking from a tyre. When we stopped the car the noise did not, so I wound down my window and braved the heat of midday without air-conditioning. In rushed a sound like a waterfall in full flow; it was the massed chorus of cicadas vibrating their tymbal organs. Each individual can output 100 decibels or more, and when hundreds are close to you it is like being at Niagara. But sound was not the only assault; in the heat of midday the gum trees were giving up their oil vapour to the sun, and the waterfall seemed to be trying to unblock its nose with a winter mixture of eucalyptus sweets or menthol rubs.

Unfortunately, there is a smell that often accompanies overseas birding, one created by open ditches carrying human waste. The black mud must ferment the ordure as it gives out sulphurous effluvia reminiscent of the mud pools and hot springs of Rotorua in New Zealand. In that particular town sulphurous mud bubbles up, heated by gasses escaping the mantle, superheating water until it forms geysers. These blow wonderfully pure-looking, but evil-smelling, steam and water all around. I've seen Maoris wrapping fish and vegetable in large leaves, tuck them into an old pair of tights and then lower the improvised cooking bag into the water and take it out only a few minutes later when the food is ready to eat. In Rotorua even the graves are built over ground and on small stone stilts to prevent the newly deceased from cooking. The open sewers of countries which can afford no better stink and the acrid smells fill your nose, but such places often offer feeding opportunities to enterprising birds. When you watch such birds you have to hold your nose or suffer the accompanying stench.

Loving birds has a downside, it becomes, for some of us, an incidental obsession. That is to say I am not actively obsessive in the way that avid twitchers are – ready to drop everything and run for their car in order to get to see a bird whether it is new for their life list or just new for the year. Such active obsession is not a natural companion to those of an indolent persuasion such as myself. I can probably do the 'dropping everything' bit, but am hardly likely to break into a run, even faced with my nemesis. My obsession is a regressive one that means that there are few, if any, aspects of life that are not bird influenced.

Take a stroll around my yard and you will find it festooned with feeders. Mouldy Nyjer seed lie in heaps in flower borders where lilies should bloom. A wonderful flowering cherry is made mundane as it is hung with ugly grey fatballs with many twigs broken by scrapping starlings, and the crazy paving is polka-dotted with birdlime. Walk my modest halls and you will find the majority hung with bird pictures and the minority lined with birding books. Every nook and cranny has avian object d'art... divers and ducks deck the den, kingfishers cram the kitchen and bedroom dressers are bedecked with barn owls.

Worse still I cannot watch a TV programme or film without searching each frame for the incidental birds. Yesterday, while struggling to unravel the plot of a murder mystery, I more easily identified city pigeons and sparrows. I find myself railing against the poor research that allows Knights of the Round Table to be seen carrying Harris Hawks or Roman Emperors to sport a menagerie housing macaws! When we incidental obsessives watch *The Africa Queen* we cannot appreciate the interplay between Hepburn and Bogart as we are stamping our feathered feet at the bird calls in the background that are clearly neo-tropical! Even the anticipated pleasure of a nature documentary can be spoiled when the 'voice over' doesn't identify a bird that is lingered upon by the camera man. Even the TV news can be belittled by our distraction. When great world events unfold that cause mayhem and suffering, my mind is likely to have wandered into observing the Black Kites soaring over a devastated Asian field or a vulture picking through the detritus of a human slum.

I should, perhaps, qualify the statement that I love birds. Indeed I do, but more accurately I love to see birds in the wild. William Blake said in his poem *Auguries of Innocence* that 'A robin redbreast in a cage puts all heaven in a rage.' It has the same effect on me and this can be a problem. Having a wide Web presence means that I get hundreds of mails every week, sometimes asking help with ID, where to take an injured bird or where to go to see a particular species. However, I also get correspondence from people who assume I am into birds as pets. I find it hard to be civil and several times have, forgive the expression, flown off the handle when, for example, people who keep parrots as pets tell me how they work for conservation. The truth is that if no one anywhere kept a bird as a pet half of the species that are at risk would be safe and sound. For every bird in a cage a dozen more died on route to the pet shop. If, as a society, we were serious about policing this problem and supporting CITES, Convention on International Trade in Endangered Species of Wild Fauna and Flora, there should be DNA checks on all imported 'pets' to ensure that their provenance is from known breeding stock rather than from the wild.

My joy is in seeing birds doing what they should in the wild, and that means marvelling at the power of a peregrine snatching a bird in flight and also marvelling at the aerobatics on an escaping prey species. I am not sentimental: birds prey on each other, but there is an apparent balance where the actions of the human world have not upset the natural order, as all too often we do. The raptor-prey conundrum was tested for me recently when I was sent a study of the diet of urban Peregrines in Exeter. They nest on the cathedral which makes collecting their prey remains easier than those on a mountain side, so a 15-year long study has taken place in order to accurately record what they eat*. Over half (55%) by weight (around 40% by numbers), of what they eat are feral pigeons. However, the study also showed that their prey included 102 species of birds as well as a few mammals (i.e. Grey Squirrel and Brown Rat), and including Noctule bats. Birds included some species that are very rare in the UK such as the Spotted Crake and others virtually never seen in the south of the UK such as the Corncrake. Peregrines often pick out night migrators as they are easy prey, so that in the autumn a large part of their diet is made up of Redwings. They also take quite large numbers of my favourite bird – the Common Swift.

British Cabinet Ministers and US Presidents, Asian Royalty and Commercial Magnates have included birdwatchers in their numbers. But this seems not to have affected their economic policies much which continue to drive for growth and deny the problem of overpopulation, making more likely the extinction of many species they purport to love.

Loving birds isn't enough. All of us who do so also need to change our daily lives, lobby those running countries and industries and empower alternative technologies if that love is not to be a hollow, selfish pleasure. Every choice we make in our daily lives has implications for the wild world at large.

* Dixon, N. & Drewitt, E.J.A. (2012) A 15-year study of the diet of urban-nesting Peregrines. *Devon Birds* 65(1), 19-30.

'*When we incidental obsessives watch* The Africa Queen *we cannot appreciate the interplay between Hepburn and Bogart as we are stamping our feathered feet at the bird calls in the background that are clearly neo-tropical!*'

M is for Mexican Jay
(Mexican Jay, *Aphelocoma ultramarina*)

Arriving in LAX – Los Angeles International Airport – I hauled my bags down endless corridors past a Janitors's cupboard from which I just heard a snatch of music – Paul Simon singing: 'I remember playin' some lead guitar, I was underage in this funky bar…And I stepped outside to smoke myself a 'Jayyyyyeeee'. '

I felt that I had arrived, not just at the airport but the centre of the universe… the land of flower power and free love, of cool dudes and rock 'n' roll. My first time overseas and I was just stopping off on my journey around the world. I was Shaft, I was Sonny Bono, I was 'The Man', high on the fact that I was where dreams are made in Californian back-lots.

On the other hand I was dehydrated, gasping for a nicotine fix and without a cent to my name. Worse, the shutters were coming down on all the airport bureau-de-change booths. As I scuttled to a window to change my small cache of limey cash, I was greeted with beaming smiles and told to 'have a good day'. However, that possibility was removed by the young cashier's intransigence – I had to have a good day without dollars as 'sorry, we are closing at this time' was proffered with a sickly smile and another urging to 'have a good day, Sir'.

Fortunately, not all Americans are automata with painted-on smiles. One of my fellow passengers spotted the deepening frown creasing my pale and sweaty brow and took pity on me by offering to buy me a drink before I set off downtown. So it was that I found myself with a cooling beer in my hand as I exited LAX's huge blow-up terminal. I was barely half way out of the door when a hand like a ham clasped my shoulder and spun me about so that I could see my face reflected in the belt-buckle of the hand's giant owner. One of LA's finest looked down at me from on high and with a voice as deep brown as his face and admonished me: 'It's an o-fence to drink intoxicating liquor on the highway.' Figuring that discretion was the only option, as valour would not survive any confrontation with the man-mountain, I slipped back inside the air-con airport. I swallowed the ice cold, but only just alcoholic, beverage barely deserving beer as a name and deposited the empty can in a litterbin – oops, I meant 'trash can'. All the while I was under the scrutiny of this seeming relative of an American double-door refrigerator. I slipped out into the hot, dry Californian air and realised that there were no free shuttles in the land of the free, and, as I had no folding stuff acceptable to a cabbie, I became the first person in the history of aviation to lug his suitcases from LAX to Downtown LA.

This journey took me through some semi-dessert where my only companions were the nodding donkeys that pumped black gold from the ground. No Cactus Wrens, no roadrunners, not even an America Crow or one of the 'buzzards' that soar above the desert in every cowboy movie ever made.

After a sweaty and exhausting walk I managed to get to the city and found myself on a Hollywood set – Wiltshire Boulevard was all I imagined it to be with glass and steel everywhere thrusting skyward, served by elevators on the outside of buildings.

It's odd how the mind goes – as I looked about me I automatically gave everything its American name, quickly translating from the English equivalent... trash can, not litter bin; elevator, not lift and instead of walking a hundred yards down the pavement, I strolled a couple of blocks along the sidewalk. Even my inner voice spoke to me with an American accent. This was 1980, and I was starring in an episode of *Starsky and Hutch*. Unfortunately, I couldn't see Huggy Bear anywhere about to tell me what 'the word on the street' was as I wandered about looking for the Greyhound 'Deepoh' – and then mistakenly tried to buy my coach tickets in a place that, it turned out, 'posted bail bonds'.

Eventually I made it to the Greyhound Bus station and queued for a ticket and then 'got in line' for the bus. This turned out to be a tad intimidating as I was the only 'Anglo' amongst many black and Hispanic people. A one day-trip to France and a week sunning myself in an all-inclusive hotel in Morocco had not prepared me for independent international travel. I was a stranger in a strange land; for the first time in my life I was a foreigner. For some odd reason when my bus arrived all but one of the other people lining up disappeared – maybe they had found the timetable as indecipherable as I. So the queue dissipated leaving just a lean and longhaired Mexican and me, worryingly he was cleaning his fingernails with a 6-inch stiletto – and I'm not talking ladies shoes! I got on the bus and looked around to find myself alone – no sign of my Mexican compadre.

Relieved and seeking safety I snuggled down immediately behind the driver and made myself comfortable, sitting back and lighting up a much-needed cigarette. The driver leant forward and pulled a microphone down in front of his face, speaking to me through it he announced: 'It is an oh-fence to smoke while the bus is in the deepoh.' I extinguished my 'fag' (mentally noting never to call it that again until I got home) and waited until the engine revved and we moved through the hangar doors and into the Californian sunlight. Relieved to be free of the sanctions of the 'deep-oh', I lit up again only to see the drivers' hand reaching for the mike once more. His melodious basso profundo boomed out: 'It is an oh-fence to smoke while still within the city limits'. Once more I stubbed out the comforter and started scanning the roadside for a sign saying that we were out of the conurbation. Forty minutes later, and so starved of nicotine that the DTs were setting in, I spotted the City Limit sign and whipped out another ciggie, lighting it with a suitable flourish. But my aplomb soon turned to apoplexy as, for a third time, the driver's hand grabbed for the mike and he intoned with unaccustomed American irony: 'It is an oh-fence to smoke while within Orange County.'

My British phlegm began to dissolve; I fought back tears of tiredness and frustration and, as only an addict can, began picking out every detail of every clue to my whereabouts. I waited for the sign that I could let the nicotine flood my very being. Eventually there it was, like a shimmering lake in the dessert of despond, a sparkling sign, picked out in angelic light: 'You are now leaving Orange County.'

I looked at the driver... he was watching me in his rear-view mirror. A trembling hand fumbled for my cigarette pack in my shirt pocket, and I almost spilled the carton's contents on the deck. Somehow I managed to draw forth a stick and tentatively place it between drawn lips. I 'stared him out' through the partition glass, darkly. Defiantly he pulled down the mike. I pushed the unlit cigarette more firmly between my lips, while watching his lips pucker and his nostrils flare more widely. The standoff lasted 30 seconds, and I imagined the camera close-up on my beads of sweat as if they were on the lip of a High Noon gunslinger.

I had barely got a spark from my Zippo when his insistent tones assaulted my ears again: 'It is an oh-fence to smoke while sitting in the first four rows of this bus'...

I scuttled to the back seat lighting up as I went and took a full lungful of smoke and blew it forward in defiance… but the driver remained quiet; he never caught my eye again, just sped on through the setting sun – clearly smoking was now allowed.

It was at this point that the stiletto-wielding Mexican staggered from the toilet at the back of the bus an hour into the journey! What dreaded disease had kept him insensible so long? Then it dawned on me – he was stoned out of his weather-beaten face. His red eyes met mine, and his lips curled – was that a smile or a snarl? He slowly pushed his hand out towards me; I trembled in horrified anticipation slowly looking down towards his hand expecting it to be gleaming with deadly steel. Instead I saw what he had proffered me, a long skinny, wet-ended reefer! His smile widened as he wheezed, 'It's great shit amigo.' I smiled and weakly shook my head with Paul Simon's words still running through my brain, realising that my new found friend had just 'stepped outside to smoke himself a 'Jayyyee'.'

$$$$$$$$$$$$

The story of my first encounter with American culture could easily end there, but let me share a further disappointment coming shortly after the bus deposited me at journey's end – San Diego. The disappointment came only after shock and horror. I was to be met from the bus by my aunt and uncle – two relatives I had never met.

My mum's sister was a GI Bride; she had married a US airman at the end of WW2 and immediately left 'Blighty' never to return. Over the years we had had a few photos with edges seemingly cut with pinking shears and displaying the colours of movies before Technicolor was invented – pale, washed out as if depleted by the war effort.

In my teenage years I had begun corresponding with my uncle. Elmer was a scientific journalist and seemed erudite and glamorous, as any Californian would to a boy growing up in 1960s Britain. He seemed to know something about everything and, moreover, he must have been a 'good 'un' as he was a total anglophile. He watched the educational channels and tuned into Mexican stations, so that he could watch soccer – a game still very much a mystery to most Americans.

So, when I stepped from the Greyhound bus onto the San Diego sidewalk I looked around for this giant intellectual uncle and my muted pastel aunt.

I was distracted by my location... I appeared to be leaning against the wall of the city gaol! Above me were barred windows through which peered forgotten men. But I heard my name called in a soft female American way and spun round to see... my mother? A heartbeat and double take later I realised that this wasn't mum but her peapod companion, Aunt Hilda. We embraced, and I was bustled into a waiting car big enough to eat an English model and consider it a snack.

By the time we had ridden out to the suburbs I was barely able to force open my eyelids as sleep deprivation suddenly kicked in... this was very nearly the day after tomorrow for me, and I apologised profusely but begged for a bed. My wish was granted but only after I had been quickly ushered about the house so that I could orientate in the night if need be. I had just a general impression of rooms all clad in plastic pretend wood panels and more TVs, in more sizes than graced our local electricity showroom.

I undressed and crawled into bed and a deep sleep. I've no idea what the local time was when slumber took me, but I guess it must have been early as I awoke refreshed to a brilliant sunny morning and searched for my watch set to LA time. It was 5.30am. Dressing quietly, I stepped out onto a neatly manicured front lawn. In one direction was a clean and tidy suburban road lined with identical one-story houses, in the other direction the cul-de-sac ended with a footpath bridge over the highway. I wandered across the bridge to see semi-dessert. I had no binoculars but could see distant raptors soaring upwards as the land gave up its heat.

I finished my cigarette and walked back to the house and was greeted by shocked faces – 'Are you completely insane?' they chorused. It took a while for the realisation to dawn in my jet-lagged mind; all this fuss was brought on by perambulation. I had walked out and into the unknown… it's just not done, apparently. Californians in those days only ever walked by car! Walking was for bums. Walking invited robbery and rape. Walking was just plain asking for it!

The day continued with coffee and waffles and lots of questions about the family doings. Later, they told me that I would be taken for a ride up to Point Loma – a lookout over San Diego Bay adjacent to an airbase where my cousin's husband was a fly-boy. As we readied for the journey another elongated shock occurred. Family topics having been exhausted, my aunt busied herself with coupon cutting and daytime TV, while Uncle Elmer and I chewed the fat – just like any good old American TV family males do. We talked about soccer and exhausted my knowledge in seconds; then about royalty but soon changed the subject when it became plain that I was a republican and my host a royalist. We talked of this and that, and gradually attitudes were revealed and I began to say less and less in the face of a horrible truth. This idol of my teenage years, this intellectual and erudite correspondent was a dyed-in-the-wool racist!

I could not believe what he was saying. He ranked races like one might stack pocket change according to denomination. Despite his Anglo-Saxon heritage, he didn't rank us white folks at the top, he had this spot reserved for Jews – clearly their place in artistic and scientific achievement was proof of their superiority, but Anglos followed on and so it went down to Hispanics and blacks who, by their under-achievement evidenced their inferiority except, of course, their superior physical prowess.

I did not know what to do. I tried to argue, but shock tied my tongue and made me stumble and fail. I guess it was fortunate that my aunt bustled in to say we should leave for our outing because it burst the debate bubble. I had a three-day stay planned and no money to do other than lodge here. They were family, and I grew up believing family comes first. Somehow I was going to have to suck it up and bite my tongue – as intellectually and emotionally impeding, as it was anatomically difficult.

So we went on the outing – a journey to bitter disappointment. Little was said as we drove out to the viewpoint and then, when there, it was so awe-inspiring as to push away the morning's exchanges. From the Point the whole city stretched out below one – across suburbia and downtown skyscrapers, then the bridge across the bay – magnificent. Man's work from a distance can almost match nature in terms of splendour, if not in grace.

Then came the final blow. Peering down, I could see that one waterfront 'block' was not built up, but that there was a patch of wet and green – even without optics I could see a lone, shining white egret picking its way through the derelict lot. Overwhelmed by this triumph of nature over man I turned to my uncle and pointed out the spot... 'Have you seen that?' I asked inviting him to share my glee that Mother Nature could sustain herself on this lonely crumb. 'Yes', he replied. 'It's a darn disgrace, but they are going to develop it soon – such a waste.' 'Such a waste' echoed in my thoughts – such a waste of intellect and writing talent lost to prejudice and now lost to me.

The standoff lasted 30 seconds and I imagined the camera close-up on my beads of sweat as if they were on the lip of a High Noon gunslinger.

I had barely got a spark from my Zippo when his insistent tones assaulted my ears again:

'It is an oh-fence to smoke while sitting in the first four rows of this bus'...

N is for Nightingale
(Nightingale, *Luscinia megarhynchos*)

Having grown up in Kent in the 1950s and started birding with my family at an early age, I was lucky enough to regularly hear Nightingales singing. All we needed to do was go to some hazel coppice near my home, at the right time of year and at the right time of the evening, and they would serenade you. The county is still a good one for these audio stars but 50 years ago they were commonplace – an expected background lullaby, not an exciting novelty. My 'tin ear' is legend – a friend once said that I was hard pressed to separate the call of a Carrion Crow from that of a Blue Tit, on a good day, down hill with the wind behind me! However, some iconic species make it easy; lying awake at 3.00am close to one of Kent's ancient Bluebell woods, it is virtually impossible to misidentify a Nightingale. I spent two years living in a mobile home, hidden in such a strip of ancient woodland during the 1990s, where each summer I was woken in the night by their beguiling trills. Rather than re-seek sleep I found myself trying to hear a repeated phrase or a bum note. Sleep evading me, I would just lie back and revel in the marvel.

If you go to one of their strongholds in England, such as Fingringhoe Wick in Essex in early May, the males sing from prominent places such as the top of a hawthorn bush, and sometimes as many as a dozen males compete for territory or mates. The song is so captivating because it seems that every phrase is uniquely new, and the throaty trills are unmistakeable (apparently there are around 300 different songs). They go on singing for a month or two but become harder to see after a couple of weeks, because they tend to vocalise from the very centre of a bush which you can circumnavigate for ages without being able to spot the songster, even though you can pinpoint the birds location through the song. You have to be very lucky to catch a glimpse of their flicking rusty tails or their heads vibrating as they sing. I don't know if this behaviour is typical or something that just the UK population does, because I have seen them singing out in the open in mainland Europe much later in the breeding season.

Nightingales are still regular at several of my local birding haunts, yet they remain a nostalgia bird for me. In my teens I read the whole H E Bates cannon at a time when 'Pop's' antics and predilections seemed innocent and wholesome. In his books it was always summer in a setting in Kent and every evening stroll through the coppiced Bluebell woods or the 'Garden of England's' orchards was accompanied by Nightingale song. In my own memories of childhood it is always summer in Kent, with birdsong echoing in the still air of long sultry evenings.

Few birds rival the vocal repertoire of a Nightingale, but some certainly make up for it in volume. Even my tin-ear can tell that a Robin is scratching out its reedy song in my garden in Spring, and I can appreciate the lilting beauty of the Blackbird that seems to sing all year, but is certainly at its best on a summer evening. However, the Wren is capable of waking you from a doze at fifty paces. Its sudden bursts of song from the middle of a tangled blackberry bush, or creeping around the pots on my patio, are one of the loudest birdcalls from one of the smallest of our birds.

Lately there is a rival. Over the last generation, one warbler has expanded into the south-east of England and beyond, and its call is even louder than the Wren. Cetti's Warblers tend to be found near water and especially in reedbeds. Hard winters may reduce their numbers, but this relatively new UK resident relentlessly pushes the envelope of its colonised territory and continues to consolidate its first foothold. In the Stour Valley in Kent, home to Stodmarsh, a reserve that has a remarkable history of rare bird finds, Cetti's have a long established stronghold. In recent years over fifty pairs have been counted on a walk from the Stodmarsh end of the reserve through to the other end at the rarity famed Grove Ferry. Even I can now recognise this call, as it shares a couple of characteristic with me; it is simple and L O U D!

Being challenged in the audio department does not mean that I am immune to song, and bird song can transport me to particular locations or at least certain habitat types. For example, the Curlew's call is always evocative; it takes me to salt marshes or high moors. The wonderfully bubbling call builds in a crescendo which forces you to listen and wait for final brief diminuendo. By the time you have heard the whole call you cannot but believe yourself to be surrounded by heather or saltmarsh and mudflats. This even holds true when the Curlew turns out to be a Starling on your neighbour's roof imitating Curlew calls.

Wood Pigeons deny their guilt in a way that forces their signature into my reluctant audio memory. 'I didn't do it, I didn't do it. I...' they say and I cannot be anywhere or at any time but by a lakeside on a summer evening with a fishing rod in my hand, trying to make out my fishing float in the dimming light. The call of a Tawny Owl always takes me to country lanes by village churchyards.

Waking up to an African dawn chorus, once experienced is never forgotten. If it is your first taste of taxa that are not known where you hale from, then it is incredibly exciting to know that almost everything you hear is a species you've never seen or heard before. I can remember on my first morning in The Gambia, my first taste of African birding, waking when the sun was only just emerging. Even though there was an ancient noisy air-conditioning unit throbbing in one corner of the room, I could hear a growing cacophony of natural noise. I dressed quietly and quickly, trying to leave Maggie undisturbed (close readers of these tales may see a pattern emerging here), and crept out onto my balcony with binoculars ready.

The first wave that hit me was heat… despite the early hour the air was thick and treacly and a good ten degrees warmer than our artificially cooled room. The second wave was sound. No humans, no insects or frogs, just a distant lapping of waves against the shore and a multiplicity of bird calls.

Doves predominated with one telling me its name; 'I-am-the-red-eyed-dove', while another was saying 'Place your bets, place your bets' and a third, which was clearly at the same casino, kept calling 'Rien de plus, Rien de Plus.' A rumbling repeated 'Ook ook ook' announced the distant presence of (I found out later) a Senegal Coucal. A delightfully familiar noise came to the surface – a Hoopoe calling out its name too: 'Hoo pooo, hoo poo.' Then I was aware of a squeaky nasal rasp being uttered by the bird that was sitting just 10 feet away in a bare tree, an as yet unidentified species of glossy starling, and on the lawn below were turquoise beauties uttering the chipping calls of Cordon Bleus. The more I tried to listen the louder it all became, but, all too soon, the songs and calls disappeared below the rising hubbub of chamber maids and breakfast cooks making ready for us guests.

The Gambia had another serenade for us at the other end of the day – the joyous singing of a group of African musicians. We have been serenaded in several African countries, and it has always been beautiful and sometimes an emotional high. In The Gambia it was a professional band, a troupe of musicians entertaining holidaymakers at the hotels and local people in open-air stadia.

I am no great 'joiner in'. The trip to The Gambia was a 'last minute cheapie' that we had booked as the most economical way to go birding there. We guided ourselves while other holidaymakers were soaking up sun and being hassled by beach vendors. Nothing is quite as disconcerting as having a local lad selling shell necklaces who, when you buy his cheapest item just to stop him pestering you, raises both thumbs and, with a perfect cockney accent, says 'luvly jubbly'! However, on one evening, after dinner, but before we became too tired to appreciate it, we decided to sit by the pool and partake of the laid-on entertainment by listening to the band. Their voices ranged from soaring sopranos to out of tune tenors, but the vivacity and enthusiasm more than made up for the variable tune carrying. Apart from the inevitable drums their musical instruments were as unfamiliar as the birdcalls. One plucked metal contraption whose name escapes me is, I know, widespread in West Africa and capable of virtuoso performances, other percussion included various tapped, scraped or rattled wooden or gourd constructions. Our band's musicianship was not up to the highest level, but collectively they managed to follow the tune and add to a melange that was not exactly harmonious but somehow pleased the ear and allowed the beat to seep into your feet. For the most part, the lyrics were completely inaccessible to us either by odd accent or strange sentence construction. One song stayed with us throughout the holiday and beyond without ever making sense to us. The chorus was 'Butter in Brazil, Butter in America, Butter in…' a long list of other countries.

In Kenya we were regaled with music during dinner at a number of the hotels and lodges with 'troubadours' accompanying themselves on guitar, wandering from table to table singing a variety of catchy songs including *Jambo Bwana* with the repeated chorus of 'Hakuna matata' which, in Swahili means 'no worries'. (This was a few years before it featured in the *Lion King* so that everyone knows it now). There was also one evening when a group of women sang to us over dinner, silhouetted against the blazing orange sky, while drums and stringed instruments played. They finished their performance just as the huge sun disappeared below the horizon, and the sky turned from orange to red, then purple and finally pitch black. Their melodies seemed to resonate even as the stars came out.

However, by far and away the most touching was in Namibia. When we arrived at the Hohenstein Lodge in the Erongo Mountains we found that our small group were the only guests. We dumped our bags in our rooms, freshened up and went to the tiny terrace looking across a rocky valley miles from anywhere. Sipping cool beers, we settled down to watch the birds visiting the small concrete pool put there to attract them in. We saw a succession of birds, many of them lifers, and the rest new for the trip, including Great Sparrow, Lesser-striped Swallow, African Red-eyed Bulbul, Familiar Chat, Chat Flycatcher, Southern Grey-headed Sparrow, Scaly-feathered Finch, Green-winged Pytilia, Violet-eared Waxbill, Red-headed Finch, Black-throated and White-throated Canary, Golden-breasted and Lark-like Bunting, and Acacia Pied Barbet as well as a Dassie Rat! In the valley we saw other birds too, Red-faced Mousebird, Mountain Wheatear, Rockrunner and Short-toed

Rock Thrush, all from the comfort of a poolside chair, beer in hand – this has to be birding heaven! (Not to be confused with any one of the places that falsely makes that claim on hundreds of websites from Quebec to Queensland!)

Our second day started out with one of the best breakfasts in Africa and turned into a red-letter day when we lucked upon a gang of Meerkats (loving birds doesn't mean that you have to ignore other taxa). It was an excellent day for birds too, and the dinner that was served that evening was also excellent. That evening the dining room was briefly visited by an extremely large green and red centipede that was perhaps six or seven inches long. Meanwhile, outside, a huge praying mantis attached itself to the glass of the patio doors giving us all a terrific close up view. Beyond, the swallows swooped to the pool until it was too dark for them to see. It was already the perfect end to a wonderful day, but it wasn't over yet.

As we chatted after dessert, the entire compliment of staff of ten or so trouped into the dining room and told us that they wanted to welcome us in their traditional way. Shyly they began to sing, but they were soon confidently into their stride and singing enthusiastically. When we applauded loudly at the end of each song it seemed to boost them even more, spurring them on to yet more intricate songs. Although we could not understand the words, the singing was in beautiful and precise harmony. It seemed to us all as if the staff had not been selected for their culinary or hospitality skills, exceptional although they were, but in order to form the most perfect of choirs.

Few birds rival the vocal repertoire of a Nightingale, but some certainly make up for it in volume.

O is for Oriental Turtle Dove
(Oriental Turtle Dove, *Streptopelia orientalis*)

I am practically an orphan – I was abandoned when a mere child at the tender age of twenty-six. My whole family decided to up sticks and move to New Zealand – they have always maintained this was no reflection on me, or my family relationships, despite my being the only member of the family to be left behind. Regardless of protests, they abandoned me in Bolton and flew as far away as it is possible to get without actually leaving the planet. If you could bore a perfectly straight shaft from Bolton through the centre of the earth you would end up in the sea well south of South Island as well as being vaporized on the way... but let's not get lost in trivial detail – I was well and truly alone in a hard cruel world (not forgetting my wife, children, in-laws and friends of course – another set of mere details, although they would probably resent that label – why ruin a good story with veracity.)

Daunted by this isolation, I planned to seek them out immediately and, just four or five years later, I had sufficient liquidity in the form of Green Shield Stamps, Embassy Tokens and pennies in the jar to travel there. A divorce left me poor day by day, but my half of the house was commuted into just enough to furnish my 'bachelor' flat or take a six-week trip... the choice was obvious, who needs chairs or rugs, cutlery, crockery or wardrobes? This was 1980 when we all slept on Habitat futons. Anyway, I had the essentials in a flat designed for newly single men – a good sound system with fully stocked drinks tray, a couple of soggy floor cushions no longer needed by a newly married friend and bunk-beds for the kids' visits. After all I only bothered the kitchen during my custody weekends, and very few utensils are needed to cook fish fingers – so hated by my children I discovered decades later! So there was no contest and I set about planning my first real overseas trip.

In those days the cheapest ticket was a 'one way round the world' deal from British Airways, and so I took advantage of this to see a little of the intervening land masses. I went out via LA (see M) and returned Singapore (see C).

It happened that this was during a period when birding had somehow slipped down my life's agenda. Why sex and drugs and rock 'n' roll should take precedence during the prime of a man's life I have no idea. All very well at the time, but I now realize that some of the finest twitches in the UK happened during a time when I was far more interested in vodka than in Vireos, and in golden-haired ladies than Golden-winged Warblers. Consequently, what I most remember from my first short stopover in Singapore was a couple of very fine meals, an outing to Tiger Balm Park and a long-haired Australian backpacker lass who asked me if she could take a shower in my hotel room.

Years later – the next time I could afford passage to the antipodes – I was accompanied by Hawk-eye (the best raptor spotter I've ever married) and had lost all interest in chasing anything but lifers (it's virtually impossible to run with a dead-leg – see W). A word of advice here… to those very many male acquaintances I have known who bird and who bitch about 'not being allowed' out very often… MARRY A FELLOW BIRDER, they are out there, even for those of us who are heterosexual!

Flying to New Zealand in one go is not recommended, if the DVT doesn't get you the boredom will! The choice of routes offers a limited number of birdy stopovers (Hong Kong for Mai Po, or Bangkok, and LA are the only viable alternatives to Singapore). On that trip Maggie and I opted for Singapore and met up with a couple of really excellent birders, the brothers Kim Seng Lim and Kim Seng Chauh who have won bird races in Malaysia, can spot the tiniest of birds at 500 paces and have written the best guide to birding in Singapore there is.

Moreover, these lads have a tremendous sense of humour and tell a good tale or two.

We took several outings with them, one into the green interior of the island preserved as forest to ensure that there is always fresh water, one to a wetland reserve and other parks and all over the island, and another over the causeway into Malaysia.

I think that Singapore is the tidiest and greenest major city in the world. Footbridges spanning major roads hang with vines, and every spare inch is filled with window boxes and shrubbery. I recall glancing out of our tenth storey window to look down upon trees lining the inner city road and watching wonderful Black-naped Orioles in the treetops.

For my outing into the green heart of town I was up way before dawn and was picked up by the brothers Kim and driven to a park where a hole in a fence allowed us to join a footpath. Before dawn broke, I had added three lifers – all owls – something I had to tell Maggie about much, much later as, while my better half loves owls above all other birds, she is not so enamoured of rising early in the morning (or halfway through the night as she calls it). Getting up a full five hours before her normal rising time is often the norm on birding holidays, and she stoically braves dawn's breaking for the most part. But having to talk, think and move at unearthly hours takes its toll, and some early starts must be forgone for her to re-charge. Back then it was unusual to tape lure birds, but this is what our guides did and that brought a hawk owl to eye-level at almost touching distance – such a stunning view meant that I mentally doubled the number of days I would have to delay the news before sharing it with Maggie.

The long walk ended where a path crossed a small stream, and we sat on the bridge watching birds awaken... an outstanding moment being when a dozen flowerpeckers of two species were scattered by a Japanese Sparrowhawk that nearly took one for breakfast.

The day we spent driving around various other Singapore hot spots started at an hour Maggie considered far from sensible, but well after the hour of 'don't be ridiculous' o'clock that I had risen at the previous day. We saw cockatoos at an army barracks, waders on a half-built runway, and Brown Shrikes every hundred metres along Changi Airport's perimeter fence.

Our day-trip across the causeway also started long before the sparrows were up... not to catch the early birds, but because so many cars traverse the causeway that there is a jam from the beginning of the morning rush hour until the end of the evening one. This is exacerbated by the differences in fuel prices that lead to people travelling one way or the other to fill up, depending on which country is levelling the most tax on petrol at that particular time. Maggie spent the hour-and-a-half journey snoozing – this is her sort of compromise, there in the flesh, but with her spirit barely peeping out from under the bedclothes.

This outing is touched upon several times elsewhere, so suffice it to say that we had a great day out in the steamy forest, which gave up many wonders, including representatives of two thirds of the world's species of tree swift sitting on one branch! But my lasting memory of Malaya was of seeing people wading up to their oxters in the turquoise waves, or precariously perched on scarily flimsy structures casting their nets, while I watched Sand Plovers danced along the strand.

My third visit to Singapore is, for those of you who have been patiently waiting, where the Oriental Turtle Dove comes in. This visit was another 'stopover' en route to Australia and NZ – the latter for a family visit and the former to see more wonderful birds. But this time we had travelling companions. Brian and Joanna have been travelling friends for over a decade. They are both disabled, but Brian uses a wheelchair as he has no use of his legs at all. This makes for some extremely fraught arrivals, as there are few hoteliers, anywhere in the world, who have a true grasp of what it means to be disabled, let alone completely unable to stand or walk. I've lost count of the times we've been shown a 'disabled' room with lips and sills into showers, basins too high to reach or too low to wheel under.

We've been met with shock when we protested that the dining room was in the basement or an upper floor with no lift! In the worse case Brian was given a room where the bed consisted of mattresses set into the floor! Travel is littered with such inconveniences... such as at Delhi airport where the gent's 'disabled' toilet was up a narrow flight of 12 stairs!

In Singapore they were shown yet another impossible room. After a protest and much explanation, they were taken to a room that was 'guarantied' to be suitable... only to find it was identical to the first one. Brian, stoical as ever, shrugged and accepted the inevitable... he could sleep and eat here, but he would have to wait for the next stage of the journey to shower. Brian has had to become expert at washing himself all over in a sitting position with nothing but a small basin and a flannel; luckily he is prepared to suffer for his art. He loves birding and birds and has been on many twitches in the UK where he has struggled across ploughed fields or negotiated sandy tracks. Fortunately, many birders offer help and he has always been prepared to be pushed or dragged, manhandled or mauled in pursuit of lifers.

Once he was bundled into the back of a jeep and propped up long enough to get his 'tick' before having to lie horizontally for the rough ride back to his wheelchair. Brian is a pathfinder, an intrepid adventurer, blazing a trail for his fellow disabled birders, enduring every indignity despite being well into his seventh decade. Once, in India, he was lifted by some hospitable Indian birders, chair and all, over the top of a kissing-gate, passed overhead from hand to willing hand – and I have the pictures to prove it... the pay off was that he got his target bird!

We have now visited five and a half continents together, and he has dipped out on remarkably few of the birds the rest of us ticked. (Having mobility issues myself, I have to say this holds true for me too; sometimes I have sat waiting for fellow birders who are walking miles to get a bird only to have it fly right by me! I can only recall missing out on half a dozen species due to being unable to trek to their limited locations.)

With a bit of thought and planning almost everything that doesn't require hacking through miles of impenetrable jungle is possible for wheelchair birders, and often National Parks, if you negotiate with, or occasionally bribe, the right people, will allow vehicular access to disabled birders – after all their wardens usually drive in themselves.

We had arranged for a vehicle with a wheelchair lift in Australia, and Brian was going to hire a manually controlled vehicle when he went off doing his own thing in New Zealand. In Singapore we were relying on the more usual method of helping Brian into an ordinary car and stowing his wheelchair in the boot until needed for actual birding.

I'd told Brian just how good my Singapore friends were as guides, and he was keen to get a few oriental species under his belt so he, I and our patient partners were outside our hotel well before first light, waiting for Kim Seng to turn up and take us off to 'walk' the roads in the hills to swell our life lists.

Despite the early hour it was already warmer than an English summer... and we were contemplating slipping back into the air-conditioned hotel atrium when the Oriental Turtle Dove finally made its appearance. One literally fell off its perch several floors above and struck Brian a glancing blow on his shoulder before bouncing onto the marble hotel steps an inch from his wheelchair to lie with its feet pointing to heaven.

'It's an Oriental Turtle Dove,' I opined peering down at the fresh corpse. Ever hopeful, Brian looked up at me... and, as if in a scene from a Monty Python sketch, said: 'I think it twitched... can I tick it?'

'I think it twitched… can I tick it?'

P is for Pardalotes
(Spotted Pardalote, *Pardalotus punctatus*)

Part One – Heard Only

There are four species of pardalote – and I haven't seen any of them. In particular I have very actively and on several occasions not seen the Spotted Pardalote!

My first encounter was many years ago when birding in northern Western Australia with the very appropriately named George Swan (see Z). This was a short but eventful leg of a trip we took to several parts of Australia. We had organized the trip ourselves and largely birded under our own steam but had decided that, as Western Australia was new to us, we would hire a guide for a couple of days in the Broome area.

The day after we arrived, George picked us up and even brought with him some 'sensible' boots for Maggie who only had sandals to wear. When he took them out of the back of the 4x4 he did what everyone does in the tropics, gave them a shake in case something nasty had crawled inside. Out from one boot rolled a stream of what appeared to be half-size mothballs... but George corrected our assumption... they were, in fact, gecko eggs!

The joys of Mangrove birding for Red-headed Honeyeater and Mangrove Cisticola, Variegated Fairywrens and all took some beating. Although from a traveller's point of view, birding there does uncover the underbelly of Australian society and how marginalised some people are. We came across several groups of native Australian women sitting in the mangroves with half-empty gin bottles in their hands, drinking away their troubles.

On other days we watched a Jabiru down to a few feet, while being devoured by voracious ants, had a close encounter with a huge feral bull and even got half a dozen lifers on a slow drive around the town! We were shown 'bowers' lined with snail and cockleshells and walked across a beach to view terns, a beach that was so hot and sunny that you had to shift from foot to foot or they burnt, and we had to shorten our visit as 'snow blindness' threatened. On one evening George took us out to look for Bush Thick-knee and other night birds. Before we caught up with the thick-knees we tried several spots, including an area of fruiting trees. To our overseas eyes this looked like an orchard until we began to go off road and disturbed a pair of ducks. However, we did not realise that this was a wetland miles from help in the dark until George drove a few feet too far and the vehicle slowly sunk down to its axels. I have had trouble driving a 4x4 on a muddy field when just one wheel gets mired and must admit to feeling a bit panicky to be so far from civilization in a sinking Landrover without means of escape. We need not have worried as the ever-resourceful George hopped out, slung a wire around a tree and used the engine's traction to calmly winch us out and pull us free of the mud.

It was terrific – even the day Maggie took a rest she became intimately acquainted with a Pheasant Coucal. However, there was one low point for me, and it was at the otherwise incredibly productive visit to Broome Sewage Works. The old settling lagoons are surrounded by a high chain-link fence and when we arrived these were completely alive with hundreds of Corellas. They lined the perimeter fence and all the shrubs and trees until a passing raptor disturbed them. En masse they rose into the air like a great white cloud but soon started to settle back down. We drove along the tracks between the lagoons while they looked on knowing we were no threat.

The works held a plethora of different waders. Every lagoon had a couple of dozen birds of three or four species and we even managed a lifer in the shape of a Wilson's Snipe. The avifauna of the area changes with the seasons and the undisturbed beaches can accumulate millions of waders in autumn, so are renowned for vagrant birds seldom seen elsewhere in Australia. We were surprised to see Yellow Wagtails and pleased to be able to add a new race to our list.

We finished our tour near the gate, which George duly got out of the vehicle to close behind us. Coming quietly back to the vehicle, he had raised his hand to indicate that I should listen as he pointed out the calls of a bird. I edged my door open and joined him by a large bush, and he whispered to me that we were hearing the calls of a Forty-spotted Pardalote. It was damn close, right where we stood in fact: the calls were coming from the hidden depths of the large grey-leafed bush which we began to circle, all the while trying to home in on the calls. We danced around this bush for a good 30 minutes with the calls continuing until suddenly they stopped, and George rushed to the far side only to say 'It's flown off high' as I joined him… I couldn't even claim to have seen a disappearing dot in the sky! Nothing annoys me more than having an 'H' on my check list (see V) – standing for 'heard only'. This was as close as I have come to seeing a pardalote of any sort. Spotted Pardalote? No, I haven't!

Part Two – the myth of the Pardalote

If you think that the Ivory Bill woodpecker sightings in Arkansas, USA, in 2005 were not an elaborate hoax motivated by the best of all intentions (i.e. to preserve the threatened habitat of primary Cyprus swamp), then you might believe in the existence of pardalotes. I was foolish enough to believe I had heard one in a bush by a poo pond in the empty north of Western Australia. But time plays tricks with the memory – perhaps that was just a dream, or an illusion brought on by desire. After all, after a couple of years of people believing that they had heard the 'kent kent' call of an Ivorybill, with a recording to prove it, scientific analysis revealed that what they had actually heard was the sound made by a vehicle going over the slats of a distant wooden bridge!

Years later I was lucky to return to the land of rattling dags, drongos and dreamtime. This trip was to the eastern side of the country and included a few days spent near the vibrant city of Brisbane with its Galah-clad parks, Blue-faced Honeyeaters-hung telephone wires and Rainbow Lorikeet-bejewelled back yards. We were fortunate enough to be in the company of Roy Sonnenburg who also, at that time, ran a B&B for birders. His 'yard' sloped down to a stream in a leafy suburb and was excellent for birds. Moreover, he was and is a really good guide (and a great bloke) who can spot a fairy wren at 200 yards, recognize the call of a bellbird from 300 yards and smell the enticing aroma of his wife's cooking at over a mile. When Roy sets out to find you a bird he is as likely to give up as leave his larger to get warm in the sun, or leave a silence unfilled with his anecdotes. When Roy smiles his whole face stays rigid and dry with only the merest gleam in his eye giving away a leg pull. His monotone threatens you with sleep, but the content of the stories threatens you with aching sides and broad grins.

We set out from his place while mist still clung to the air, and the streets were empty but for yesterday's longest staying partygoers. Before breakfast we had tucked a myriad of fairy wrens and grass wrens under our belts and added another three dove species to our life list. Before we were allowed to tuck into lamingtons and cold drinks we had fed three species of parrot as they flocked out of the bush to surround the car park at O'Reilly's. Brian had sat with a King Parrot on his head and two Rosellas on the arms of his wheelchair, and I had posed for the statutory snaps of 'a man trying to feed birds with an armful of parrots'.

We had waited while a coach disgorged the noisiest Japanese tourists ever heard, watched them snake along a boardwalk in thrall to their guide, then snake back aboard the bus and away without ever seeing the Brush Turkeys and Eastern Whipbirds that called all around us. Before our breakfast we had crept about in the undergrowth, adding all manner of lifers to our lists before the 16 kilometre back, a road that was, Roy assured us, the easiest place in Australia to see pardalotes.

We set off with high hopes and life lists to the fore and were soon clocking up new birds; our first was a Treecreeper at the spot that Roy had told us was his 'guarantied' pardalote stop. We stopped here a while with flasks of coffee waiting in vain for pardalotes to appear. 'Not to worry', said Roy, as his 'second best spot' was just round the corner and that he 'got pardalotes here, nine times out of ten'. On we went, but the pardalotes had clearly decided that we were a birding party too much and had decided to disappear into another part of the bush. 'No worries,' iterated Roy, 'Pardalotes are always on the move, but I'm pretty sure we'll pick them up at the next spot.' The next spot was a high lookout over a deep wooded valley where we could see fruit pigeons and hear parrots calling. When pardalotes once more disappointed us, Roy was still full of optimism. 'I usually get some a bit further down the road,' he re-assured us.

Twenty minutes later and two more spots had proved pardalote-free. Roy's tone was getting a little more subdued when he said, 'I have had them just a bit further down the road', as we moved off again. Further down the empty road his voice was quieter and getting strained, and his chin was further into his chest when he said, 'I once had one in the next stand of Eucalyptus', so on we drove into a fine area of open woodland with the smell of eucalyptus beginning to fill the warming air. With that stand behind us, Roy's twinkle had diminished to a mere glint. He then announced in a hopeful tone, 'I've been told about them being seen a bit further down.' Half a kilometre later, when that spot turned out to be fruitless, his despondent voice pleaded 'Rumour has it, that pardalotes, used to be seen somewhere along this track.'

As we broke free from the trees into the sunlit meadows, Roy's voice could only just be heard above the sound of the 4x4's engine. 'I would have liked to have shown you some pardalotes today, but the sad truth is they HAVE VERY RECENTLY BECOME EXTINCT.'

I still have yet to see a pardalote!

'I would have liked to have shown you some pardalotes today, but the sad truth is they HAVE VERY RECENTLY BECOME EXTINCT'

Q is for Quail
(Common Quail, *Coturnix coturnix*)

I have heard very few quail and seen even less. Most quail are elusive, although some 'sing' from a prominent perch. I think that the first species I ever saw was in New Zealand, although it was an introduced species... California Quail. These are a very attractive species with a crest that hangs forward from the top of their heads like a fishing lure being dangled in front of a fish. I saw one in my sister's seaside garden on a visit there and over several weeks kept seeing them disappearing into long grass until one slowly walked across her lawn giving me great views. It was some time before I heard their call.

In the 1980s, my mother dabbled with driving. After one 'lesson' from my dad, which ended in shouting, sulks and threats of divorce, mum decided on 'proper' lessons. After several such lessons from a qualified tutor that ended in shouting sulks and threats of legal action, mum hung up her driving gloves. However, before the lessons had started, the fancy first took her that she should persuade dad to buy her a car so she could 'practice'.

New Zealand, at the time, had no car manufacturer at all. This meant that all New Zealand cars were imported and hence expensive. New cars attract a hefty tax, so, in those days, there was a roaring trade in imported second-hand cars. Most of these came from Japan where the regulations are so tough that cars have a short life before they are more likely than not to fail inspection. After a couple of years many were exported to countries that do not make their own. Australia does make cars; Ford manufactures there under the name of an extinct Aussie firm, Holden. These cars are reliable and tough, which they need to be given the rough back roads there. They have a long life span, and so many also ended up exported to New Zealand that has similarly testing road surfaces. Being financially challenged, my parents' household could not really afford to be a two-car family, but dad had a long history of giving in to his beloved, so searched out the most affordable machine he could. So mum became the proud owner of a vehicle that she had never driven, and never did drive. The ancient Holden was mostly ignored between annual inspections but for ensuring that the tires did not perish, nor the rust get too tight a hold.

Thus it was that, on one of my antipodean trips I had the welcome freedom of a car to drive while there. Mum was happy to see the old girl given a run out, and dad was happy that his errant son could not possibly bend his pride and joy.

Driving in New Zealand, apart from in and around Auckland, is, in terms of traffic, like driving in the UK in the early 1960s. I think that, in those days, there were more motorway miles in Rutland than in the whole of New Zealand. Apart from major roads many roads out of town were not tar-sealed. Crushed rock surfaces that are not tar-sealed are fun to drive as they are mostly empty, and a country spin is like a cross-country rally in more affluent countries. If you drive slowly, say between 30 and 40 miles an hour, nothing untoward is likely to occur. However, if you allow the speed to creep up into the 50s and beyond, you kick up a lot of dust, are in danger of sliding off at corners and your wheels throw out dollar-size bits of gravel at all angles. Even so, it was terrific fun to slide around corners and bound along with loud 1970's rock music blaring from the open windows.

I set off birding one day, under strict instructions from mum not to take the vehicle above 40 unless there was good tarmacadam beneath the wheels. Without the assurance of sat nav, but having a pretty good sense of direction, I explored the back roads of 'northland' looking to boost my meagre NZ bird list. For the most part there was little evidence of extant human life bar the gates I drove past every so often bearing large numbers referring to their milk collections. New Zealand may have more than ten times the number of sheep than they do people, but they also grow an awful lot of cows. Dairy produce is, I think, their second largest export. There is plenty of evidence that man has transformed the whole landscape. Huge dairy farms have created pasture where once was forest, marshes and scrub. Now only small patches of native bush remain in the rolling hills and flatlands. Not only have European settlers cut down the Podocarps (New Zealand conifers) and Pungas (tree ferns) and mined the land for the gum that used to run off the trees, but they also brought rats and possums, foxes and stoats, making life hard, if not impossible, for the native avifauna. Worse yet, missing their homes, they brought with them a range of birds that have spread out across the country, stealing the niches of native species, many of which are ground nesters and poor flyers.

So, as I slipped, slid and swung along the lanes, there was little to see apart from Skylarks and Goldfinches, Blackbirds and Yellowhammers, as well as ubiquitous House Sparrows and Mynas. I did see a few more interesting imports such as colourful Eastern Rosellas and several widespread natives such as the Pukekos that occupy the moorhen niche and plenty of fantails. Occasionally I came across a fat New Zealand Pigeon or heard the plaintive calls of Tuis'.

Thus it was that, lulled by miles of empty road, the thrill of free motoring and the saxophone riffs of *Baker Street* blaring inside my metal cocoon, I encountered another vehicle, and it was nearly head on! As I slewed around a corner at 50 miles an hour, a similarly lulled motorist was slewing around the same corner from a different direction. We both braked as hard as we could and tried to steer away from a collision. Our joint manoeuvres would have seemed to an observer to have been the rehearsed choreography of two stunt drivers because we came to a standstill both at right angles to the road about three inches apart with our wound-down drivers windows parallel. We looked at each other, smiled, shook each other's proffered hand and, with no words exchanged, carefully drove away. A few yards on I pulled to the side of the road and silently thanked whatever birding gods were protecting me. It was at this point that I nearly died of shock when a California Quail called loudly from the roadside Ti-trees making me jump so high I banged my head on the car roof.

It seems that California Quail pine for the cities of the North American mid-west, as they shout 'Chic-ag-o' very, very loudly! I saw two other species of quail before I ever saw a European one. On a walk around Tiritiri Matangi (see G) a covey of Brown Quail, an Australian species, ran along the path before me as if I was a mother goose shepherding her goslings. Many years later, in Kenya, I saw a tiny 'button quail' no bigger than a fat sparrow sunning itself on a path just before sunset.

During my twitching years I had heard a number of 'Common Quail'. These birds have a wonderful call of 'wet-my-lips', usually heard late on a summer evening. Not only is the call so loud that they can 'whisper across seven fields', but it is strangely ventriloquial too. Many times I have thought that I am virtually on top of the bird only for the next call to emanate from 50 yards away. I assume that their mates are not fooled and know just where to meet up. Indeed they must do so as this odd fellow migrates north from Africa to southern Europe in early spring and raises a family, then often migrates to northern Europe in early summer to do it all over again!

Ironically, having chased calling Common Quail all over the south-east of England, I saw my first one in South Africa! While out birding, we had stopped the car so that our guide could go and pick up a dead Puff Adder on the road to better show us its markings (I never want to be that close to a live one). As he threw the corpse into the roadside, a Common Quail burst from cover and flew an inch above his head before banking round and diving for the long grass again. I eventually managed to remove the 'heard only' from my UK list when I lucked upon a small family group on farmland in late summer. However, none of the above was the inspiration for this section, this was a quail of an altogether different sort that occurred in Gibraltar.

My son Ash took to birding around the time he started secondary school, and, for some years, the only books he ever read were field guides! In his early teenage years, whenever I could, I would include him in birding outings, and it was clear that he had inherited a love of wild things in general and birds in particular. His mother was also interested enough to not mind taking him on the odd trip too, so he began to build a UK list that, these days, despite him hardly getting the chance to bird, is still longer than mine. But, before he got into twitching with birding mates, he had his first overseas birding jaunt with Maggie and me.

I had long wanted to see a Great Bustard, and the cheapest reliable way to do so was to take a package holiday in the Algarve, Portugal's southernmost province. We picked a spot near the Spanish border that also held the possibility of some other wished for birds along with the chance to motor down to the Cota Doñana and maybe on to Gibraltar for the sheer fun of seeing the rock. Within a few days of arriving we had seen plenty of birds that were lifers for all three of us. These included Black Stork, Azure-winged Magpie, Great Spotted Curlew, Lesser Kestrel and, of course, both Great and Little Bustards. Having already found the majority of our target species, we thought we'd book a night or two in a Gibraltar hotel so that we could have a couple of days in southern Spain by slowly birding our way down, spend a full day exploring the rock itself, then motor slowly back to the Algarve.

A couple of hours into Spain and our plan was already vindicated by wonderful views of dozens of Griffin Vultures soaring over the high hills and other goodies like Black-shouldered Kite along the way. Before crossing the border onto the rock, we managed a few hours around the Delta adding some wonderful birds including Spanish Imperial Eagle, Bluethroat and Glossy Ibis among many others. We even managed to get our hired car stuck in the sandy streets of El Rocio during a sudden downpour while taking a quick look at this remarkable little town of white walls, blue tiles and hitching posts for the horses.

Crossing into Gibraltar from the mainland was nowhere near as straightforward as one might think, but we managed to do so eventually and even found our hotel quite quickly… it turned out to be rather rundown and of the sort one finds all too often in English seaside resorts. Worn carpets, shabby mismatched furniture and grey bed linen did not inspire us, but we were right opposite a reasonable restaurant and in sight of the cable car, so there was some compensation. Next morning we made use of both, breakfasting and then 'climbing' to the top of the rock the easy way.

It was certainly interesting to see the way one side of the rock has been engineered to capture water and to sit in the sun being pestered by the famous 'apes'. Laying back, we did see birds migrating into Europe from Africa, mostly White Storks, but we did see one Black one soar overhead too. Seeing few birds around us apart from Yellow-legged Gulls, we decided to walk around a bit which proved a good move as we got great views of Blue Rock-thrush. After a while we realised that we had begun to descend and came to a fork in the road and discussed which was the best route. Ash decided he would take one way while we took another and that we would meet at the cable car at the foot of the rock. Our way eventually led to a cable car stop, so we hopped aboard and rode down to the base. An hour or more later there was still no sign of Ash as we enjoyed an ice cream in the shelter of the cable car pylons – avoiding the strengthening breeze. Eventually we decided that we should head back up to see where Ash had got to and went over to the ticket office.

I asked for two more tickets, but the chap in the booth shook his head and said: 'Sorry, we are now closing the cable car as it is getting very windy.' Taken off guard, I gasped, 'You can't do that, my son is still up there!' 'What's the boy's name?' he asked. 'I'll ask the operator to look out for him and get him back down.'

As I told him that my son was called Ashley he spoke into a radio passing this information on to his colleague. A few minutes later he turned back to me to say: 'Don't worry, my colleague has found him and is bringing him down now.' Maggie and I stood at the foot of the cable car waiting for him to arrive. For a few minutes, as the car arrived, we could see Ash glaring at us from the cable-car window.

This, dear reader, is where the less common quail came in... as he stepped off the car, his penetrating glare and white knuckles particularly contrasting with his red face made me quail. Later, when he was calm enough to talk to me he explained how he and some other tourists had been told to wait in the car before coming down and then they overheard the operator calling to anyone who was about... 'Has anyone seen a little lost boy up here, as his worried parents are down below waiting for him, his name is Ashley.' My six feet tall 'little boy' had to explain to the operator and his fellow travellers that he was that little lost child!

...as he stepped off the car, his penetrating glare and white knuckles particularly contrasting with his red face, made me quail.

R is for Rose-coloured Starling
(Rose-coloured Starling, *Sturnus roseus*)

Many of we birders experience a hiatus in birding. Intervening between the nerdy years of teenage birding and the obsessive years of twitching or steadfast patch birding may nestle a year or two where we 'get a life'. For the majority of us this will be all about sex and drugs and rock 'n' roll. I use this as a generic term rather than implying that birders all have a history of illegal opiate use or the abuse of legal inebriates, although I have yet to meet a tea-total birder. I merely mean that birding does sometime, at a certain age, take a poor second place to finding a mate and bringing new birders into the world. Sometimes, unfortunately, birding even has to give way to the world of work. However, generally, for anything other than casual dabblers in avian pursuits, these 'wasted' years come to a close and we can take our rightful places in the queue to see the rarity that just turned up on the local gravel pit.

When we reach this mark of maturity we can then look back at all the missed opportunities and cry ourselves to sleep. I know of many a birder who has jetted off with his or her new spouse to some exotic clime and honeymooned without ever once taking note of the lifers that abound all around – shocking, eh? Family holidays spent on a beach rather than at a nearby sewage works or touring bars in Magaluf rather than scouring the municipal dump for rare gulls, Cattle Egrets and vultures just bring shame on to the whole birding community.

I admit to having hardly birded during the years of my first courtship, marriage and subsequent rug-rat raising. Even after the first wave of nappy backup and sleepless hours of floor walking with a teething child gripped overly tight with my own tight teeth clenching, I did not get back into the proverbial saddle for some years. I have no idea why I thought that 12-hour days spent in social work, charity management and other people-oriented services were somehow important enough to be completely unaware that there was a Golden-winged Warbler in the car park of the supermarket near my childhood school bus route. Nevertheless, it was so. I spent many off-work hours discussing politics, human rights and other trivial pursuits instead of polishing my binoculars and waxing the Barbour, ready for the pleasures of sea watching in a gale. I went on protest marches rather than take a good long walk along the shoreline getting a sobering soaking while waiting for an autumn migrant to peep above the Sea Holly. I hesitate to admit it but, by the time I realised the error of my ways, I found myself with out-of-date optics, a dog-eared field guide and outdoor wear more suitable to a WW2 route march than a wet weather twitch.

During those years I took several holidays without even packing any binoculars. I shudder now to think how stupid I was to go to Tunisia *and* Morocco without being able to identify any birds except some far off Flamingos. My tally for Greece and Turkey combined is an Olive Tree Warbler in Corfu, one Little Egret in the lagoon and a Middle Spotted Woodpecker that practically joined me for a breakfast of goat's cheese, honey and olives under a mulberry tree in Ölüdeniz, Turkey. I even walked around Singapore and a rubber plantation in Malaysia without a single tick.

I can confess these transgressions only because there have been many seasons since spent in devout repentance. Travel, both foreign and domestic, were the triggers to re-ignite the flame of a birding passion that never quite cooled.

My dad had been the person who fostered my infant interest in nature and, on a visit to him in New Zealand, that tiny ember was fanned back into a small but steady flame. He took me out to some mudflats where Pied Shag, Black-winged Stilt and Banded Plovers roamed. Seeing new birds with an old forgotten pair of binoculars that I had actually bought for him got me started on a New Zealand list. On my stopover in LA on the journey home I managed no less than 36 species from the hotel bedroom, including, would you believe, an Anna's Hummingbird and a Painted Redstart. By the time I was back in the UK I was a born-again birder.

It was my custom, as the manager of a type of community centre, to arrange training weekends in the country for my staff, and some of us began taking short breaks together during holiday periods. It was thus that I began watching kites in Wales, Dartford Warblers in Dorset and Golden Eagles on Skye. Soon I was upgrading optics, buying sensible boots and dipping back into the vicarious pleasure of a well-illustrated field guide. Those not bitten by the birding bug could probably have left it at that. I knew plenty of people who enjoyed seeing birds on their country walks who could just as easily take a three-hour lunch in a nice country pub as hike further over the hill in the hope of spotting some different species. Most of my friends were happy to commune with nature but even happier to co-habit with a pint of 'Old Speckled Hen' or, indeed, the landlady of the Duck or Grouse.

I began to see such weekends away as opportunities to re-start my UK life list and often resented the diversion of the companionship of non-birders. My suggested outings were increasingly dictated by available habitat types and likely target species, rather than by the likelihood of inglenook fires and oak-beamed lounge bars. The final nail in the coffin of sociability was meeting someone who had never seen a woodpecker in the wild and really wanted to. I met, and fell for a birder in the making, and she has been my constant companion ever since. In nearly a quarter of a century we have hardly been apart for more than two days at a time and are always happy to be in each other's company twenty-four seven. The odds of meeting your soul mate, despite opportunities afforded by internet dating and personality profiling, seem diminishingly small. Meeting one by chance is even less likely, but that she is a keen birder too I still find hard to believe myself. What is more, no one is better at spotting high-flying raptors than Maggie. Almost every trip we have ever taken with a group she has managed to find a lifer for the tour guide! There has only ever been one small fly in this elixir – in-laws!

Please do not think that I had anything other than a terrific relationship with my in-laws. They were grateful for any small thing I ever did for them, and my mother-in-law, even I can admit, spoilt me rotten!

The Benidorm Years

For many years my parents-in-law holidayed in that birding anathema, Benidorm. For any one who has never visited this over-populated blot on the landscape, Benidorm is a huge conglomeration of high-rise hotels on the Spanish coast where half of northern Europe seems to spend the summer turning brown twixt the soft sand and the relentless sun. The Spanish flavours and tints are very much muted by the plethora of English 'pubs', German eateries and hundreds of small shops selling cigarettes and booze and souvenir knickknacks. You can spend an entire two weeks never eating anything that is not available at your local Tescos nor hardly hearing an accent unlike your own.

The fly nose-dived into my ointment when my in-laws had cut their ties with their old friends and yet did not feel confident holidaying alone. If we are lucky enough to advance in years yet remain fairly spry we will all, no doubt, want to go on doing the things we have always done. Even so, there will come a time when the spirit is willing but the flesh is either frail or fearful of being taken ill. Falling sick at home can be hard, but, for many, the thought of being ill overseas is very daunting. So it came to pass that my in-laws still wanted to spend a few winter weeks in the mild Mediterranean, yet they were held back by the worry of being stranded by some medical emergency. They hit upon a solution – Maggie and I could share their sojourn. We could holiday at their expense while they could feel safe in the knowledge that if 'anything happened' we could take care of things. Win-win; they announced with glee!

We could have been harsh and honest and told them just how much we hated the idea of packaged Spain, stuck with a million other sun worshipers, but we were either too soft or too cowardly. Thus it was that we found ourselves, for a number of years, using up our holiday allowance chaperoning my in-laws among the fleshpots of the Costa Blanca. I guess that despite aging we all tend to enjoy the things we did in our heydays. Often we assume that what 'old' people do is the same generation upon generation and that somehow we will all transform into old people and quite suddenly enjoy music from the 1940s, tea dances and vegetables boiled to vapour! My teenage years in the 1960s and salad days in the 1970s mean that the tunes and mores of that era are the ones I still enjoy having entered my seventh decade. My mobile phone plays *Baker Street* and my Internet avatar shows me with hair to my shoulders in a headband wearing a jacket covered in peace patches and wearing shades. This anachronistic portrait reflects my current likes and dislikes. My in-laws tastes reflected their prime too; they chose a hotel that reflected those likes and dislikes and we were assumed to share them.

So each year, for several years, we spent two weeks eating food that catered to an English palette of a certain age and being entertained nightly by a variety of dire performers. Our particular favourite was called Nitty Colsar. I have no clue where he hailed from, but he sang a collection of British and American songs by the likes of Al Jolson and Tom Jones but without being able to pronounce the words properly because, I am pretty sure, he had no idea what they meant. His voice was over breathy and not always in key, and it sounded as if he had learned the words phonetically and was unable to translate them. This was, in fact, entertaining, but not, I am sure, as he intended. It was very funny, and it was also a great challenge to try and work out what the words he was trying to sing actually were! Twice a week there was a comedy spot always occupied by comics who had clearly been long retired from a Butlin's or a Pontin's Holiday camp and whose jokes were, shall we say, unreconstructed – from an era when all sorts of 'isms' had not been coined. It varied from juvenile to puerile and from unfunny to downright offensive.

We always stayed at the same hotel, which had better remain nameless less I overstep the bounds and slag it off too much. Views from the room varied from the back of another hotel through to courtyards and streets. Birding from there was confined to White Wagtails and Black Redstarts that found titbits blown into the gutters or took a drink for leaky aircon units.

Our days were sometimes spent driving out to the lemon groves or to find a nice waterfront café in the local small towns where one could enjoy the coffee and watch the waves. Often Maggie would be required to shop or walk the beach promenade with her folks, while I, through papal dispensation, was allowed to hide in our room working on my laptop.

Very occasionally we were allowed to take a few hours to drive out of town to see if we could find any birds. At one end of the resorts there is a back road up into wooded hills where we managed to add a few ticks to our Spanish list in the scrubland such as Serin and common woodland species, including Firecrest. Further into small fields we found one spot alive with Black Redstarts that seemed, like us, to be overwintering as we identified four different sub-species ranging from birds that were very similar to Common Redstarts through to very dark and dull ones. On this little patch we also saw a few more interesting birds like Hoopoes or tits, finches and the occasional woodpecker. In one place a Southern Grey Shrike was guarantied.

Behind the town, during the years we were there, they were working on a huge visitor attraction that combined a zoo with a pleasure park – Terra Mitica. During the construction it was also not bad for birds and on one memorable day we even found a Black Wheatear – a lifer! Whenever we could we found other things for the folks to do that necessitated getting out of town, but we never quite managed to get to a wetland (apart from a rubbish-strewn pool in a town along the coast where a few dull flamingos roosted) or into the mountains and so had to satisfy ourselves with what birds there were locally. I also managed occasionally to sneak out in the early mornings or dusk to satisfy the inner birder.

The Black Wheatear was a one off, and we rarely saw anything of great note. Just like at home where I have rarely turned up a bird worth sending in a record for. One evening I was looking out of our room window at the palm trees behind the hotel, watching as hundreds of sparrows and Starlings trooped into their noisy night roost. An odd starling suddenly caught my eye and I grabbed my bins. Yes! It was an immature Rose-coloured Starling! I barely had time to punch the air in triumph when a full adult joined it! Two quite rare birds for the heart of this Iberian metropolis, I thought. A couple of days later I managed to find who to report it to, but it was not until after our return home that I discovered that I had actually spotted the sixth and seventh Rose-coloured Starling ever recorded in Spain! I've never found anything remotely this rare in the UK. Thanks Bertie and Millie – overwintering with your in-laws can bring birding joy after all.

In nearly a quarter of a century we have hardly been apart for more than two days at a time and these days are happy to be in each other's company twenty-four seven. The odds of meeting your soul mate, despite opportunities afforded by internet dating and personality profiling, seem diminishingly small. Meeting one by chance is even less likely, but that she is a keen birder too I still find hard to believe myself.

S is for Spiderhunter
(Little Spiderhunter, *Arachnothera longirostra*)

Birding has taken Maggie and me all over the world from the temperate north through the sweating hot tropics and to milder southern climes, as well as most points in between and, for many years, I managed to play a role that went virtually unnoticed. I sought neither praise nor acclamation; my task could only be achieved in such secrecy as would satisfy any 'black ops' unit of the CIA or MI6.

Maggie is an arachnophobe. By this I do not mean that she doesn't like spiders, nor even that she is frightened of them – I mean she has a deep, abiding and unshakeable terror of spiders.

Now, as with most people, spiders seem to me to be small visitors from another planet having no proper place in our world. I don't particularly like them. I'd go so far as to say that I shudder when one of those large and hairy types walks nonchalantly across the carpet when the nights start to draw in, presumably on its way from the wide world to some crevice where it can bother the borrowers. Once, when cleaning out my dad's pond in New Zealand, a great grey and hairy water spider popped up and ran across my hand causing me to instantly flinch in disgust and not a little anxiety. I remember walking through some long grass in the olive groves of Greece and emerging with a spider covering my entire kneecap and, once again, this made me shudder as I brushed it off in fear and disgust. These are, I imagine, average responses. Most people will relate to this and only a small percentage will enjoy the company of arachnids or be prepared to tango with tarantula. Even so, we of course recognise their place in the tapestry of the eco-sphere. Despite our dislikes we leave them be and hope they have the same respect for us.

But Maggie doesn't shudder nor does she flinch in fear... she panics and is frozen in abject terror unable to avoid the object of her fear. She fears further such encounters, terrified that if she actually touched one her heart would stop.

Much of the world does not understand the difference between a fear and a phobia. I grew up knowing the difference as my mum had a phobia about heights. If my dad drove along a road flanked by ditches with sheer drops of as little as three feet, mum would panic. To get her up the stairs into the airplane when they emigrated took 16 large gin and tonics; a further two dozen were needed to sedate her during the trip – she never flew again. She could get vertigo on a carpet with a thick pile.

So I have been sensitised to such problems and have done my best over the birding years to ensure that Maggie is not in close proximity to spiders. It is my duty to inspect our hotel rooms and remove anything larger than a money-spider from it. For, although the bigger they are, the more freaked out Maggie becomes, any spider, even one the size of a penny is still the object of fear if it occupies any space that Maggie does not want to share. If a spider of virtually any size were to walk across her path in the great outdoors she would not flinch. However, put the same beast into a ballroom with her and she shudders and moves to the far end; put one in her bedroom and she needs a strong sedative.

Phobias are as real as they are irrational. It matters not that some spiders can kill with their venom and others are unable to pierce the skin, it matters not whether it is a hairy giant or a penny-sized baby, all are anathema to my spouse. When in Malaya we saw the Little Spiderhunter she immediately wanted to adopt the bird as a permanent companion and willing helper in her spider eradication programmes.

Confronted with a web, hung high in a tree, pulsating with a thousand spiderlets, Maggie can walk by… but as aforementioned, put her in a room with a currant-sized arachnid and she is paralysed. So every morning when we are away I am up early enough to check the bathroom out and shake our towels lest some eight-legged critter has taken up overnight residence.

This system worked well across nearly 20 years and five continents where I was able to clear rooms well before any intruder could be seen. This is no mean feat when you consider that, over the years, we both encountered many more acceptable roommates such as geckos, golden cockroaches, hornets, stick insects, praying mantids and frogs to no ill effect. She wasn't bothered by any of these and even enjoyed one or two of these creatures… like the chameleon that followed me into our room in Namibia and had to be shepherded out in case we accidentally trod on it.

Maggie never knew about the black and hairy plum-sized denizen of the night that I dispatched in Trinidad, nor the many lesser spiders that I have washed down plugholes or ushered out of windows. Only after the event was she aware of one of the closest encounters.

In The Gambia we were sitting in a Pizza place pondering the oddly worded menu when I noticed the form of a hand-sized and very hairy spider clinging to the underside of the table. Luckily I hadn't ordered, so when I took Maggie's hand and announced that I didn't really like the place after all she was in no way reluctant to leave. She had twigged that there must be a lurking spider, just not its dimensions.

One of the ways we have managed to avoid them is in the close attention we have paid to the accommodation we have used, especially in the tropics. Wherever possible we look for air-conditioning, not so much for the cooling effects (although I for one welcome them) as for the fact that such rooms must have no open windows, air-vents or gaping gaps around doors if they are to work efficiently. We never book into a hotel or lodge if it has a thatched roof with no intervening ceiling… thatch is spiders' heaven.

All good things, they say, must come to an end. So, after a virtually trouble-free double decade, when it went wrong it did so in spades.

Many people would have loved the lodge we stayed at in Zambia. The fact that a Tchagra was nesting in the open-air foyer would have thrilled most, but for Maggie it was a harbinger of impending doom! When we were shown our 'cabin' her heart almost stopped there and then. It was nearly dark and we were hours away from any alternative, so knew we were trapped. The cabins had hard earth floors and the bamboo walls had more gaps than the teeth of the Pogues' lead singer. The doors didn't just 'not fit', they were hardly 'fit for purpose' as there was a four-inch gap at the bottom. Right at the centre of the room a bare bulb swung in the breeze, its 20 watts barely piercing the gloom. There was but one redeeming feature, the bed had a full-size mosquito net with very few moth holes so offered shelter to Maggie's storm- tossed fears.

She insisted that the net was tucked under the mattress and our clothes and anything needed in the night was piled onto the bed safe from intrusion. The downside of this arrangement was rolling over in the night onto my boots, a torch and Maggie's handbag. The minor upside was that the room's filigree walls meant that there was some cool air to ease the breath in the otherwise oppressive heat. So we tried to sleep despite the cacophony of night noises from the tropical insects and piping frogs.

A few hours in a loud whistling just outside the hut woke us up. Then the banging began like someone drumming on an upturned cast iron cooking pot. Only the next morning did we find out why this performance was repeated several times during the night. Apparently elephants had come out of the forest to eat the crops of the local villagers who spent hours clashing saucepans together, whistling loudly and drumming on an upturned cast iron cooking pot to encourage them to leave! This interruption pales into total insignificance compared with the entertainment later in the night. Maggie had heard some rustling under the bed and sought out our torch and shone it on the floor – there in the light was the biggest, hairiest, reddest spider either of us has ever seen... about the size of an outstretched hand! I was woken by her shrieks and pleas of 'Kill it! Kill it!' and had to leap into action despite being totally unprepared, half asleep and completely naked. I was assigned the task and handed the only weapon we had – a plastic coke bottle.

As adumbrated earlier, I do not pretend to be fond of spiders, particularly big, red, hairy ones! I most certainly did not relish the prospect of a naked encounter with the foraging daddy of all arachnids. However, Maggie made it quite clear that there were no options and continued to remonstrate with me to practice arachnocide. So there I was, dancing from one foot to the other stabbing at a beast in the night with an ineffective weapon – when I tried to push the spider into the next world it pushed back. Eventually I had the thing sufficiently beaten into submission to deliver the coup de grâce and was handed my boot for the purpose!

Later we were told that these beasts were not biters and did not really attack but frightened many people. These spiders were not happy in the sun and when caught out in the sunlight near a person, they try to get into the shadow and then people think that they are trying to 'get them'. Not that this was relevant; Maggie cares not one whit for the arachnid's motives – its very presence is an abomination she will not tolerate, however benign its intentions.

Having suffered this assault on her sensitivities, she was in no mood to accept the next lodge we arrived at – one look at the thatched roofs of Drotsky Cabins in Botswana and she burst into tears of rage and frustration. Moreover, when we entered our cabin, high in one corner was a monster black and yellow spider probably waiting to pounce. Lucky for me, as I badly wanted to see the birds the area has to offer, the owners knew where they could get hold of a mosquito net at short notice, even repaired its small tears and erected it over Maggie's bed, so we were able to boat up the Okavanga and tick off Carmine Bee-eaters, Pel's Fishing Owl, Slaty Egret and many other wonders.

This experience has made subsequent trips much harder to plan, and I have to seek even greater assurances that all our accommodation is as spider-free as it is possible to be. No one can guarantee that there will be no encroachment, but at least we can insist that every room has a proper ceiling and glass in the windows. It is amazing how little notice the average tour guide takes of such things. Even lodge owners are often ignorant of their own properties – as with all things in life, one has to experience a problem to be aware of how to overcome it.

Guides are not always helpful as they, like many other mortals, cannot appreciate the depth and breadth of a phobia, and they are crass enough to think it funny to say 'Look out, there's a spider!' when none are present... naturally, we never travel with such people a second time.

On the other hand, there are guides who have become great friends of ours because of their sensitivity. I remember in India a friend, Mohit, whose company guided us, putting his finger to his lips as he turned up on our balcony with a large stick, which he pretended to be walking with. He then suggested that Maggie might like to go into the shade of her room... she caught on quick enough to witness him using the stick to dispatch a spider on the balcony's ceiling.

Despite meticulous research and seeming ample re-assurance, we encountered problems the very next trip we went on – to Sri Lanka. The first place we were booked into, described as luxury forest chalets, turned out to have no roof on the bathroom and lattice airbrick all around the main room for ventilation. As it could not be spider-proofed we were moved elsewhere. Amazingly the place we moved to was only 10 minutes away and actually cheaper with nicely sealed rooms replete with air conditioning.

Thinking back, many of the places we have stayed at could have given access to other critters, not just spiders. One of the things that keeps me sensitive to Maggie's fears is the thought that such open air rooms would offer no barrier to snakes – an intrusion from one of these would surely freak me out!

I was woken by her shrieks and pleas of 'Kill it! Kill it!' and had to leap into action despite being totally unprepared, half asleep and completely naked. I was assigned the task and handed the only weapon we had - a plastic coke bottle.

T is for Tengmalm's Owl
(Tengmalm's Owl, *Aegolius funereus*)

Dr Peter Gustaf Tengmalm (1754-1803), a Swedish physician and naturalist, was among the most meticulous and knowledgeable ornithologist of his generation… one might almost say he had a wisdom that is a characteristic traditionally assigned to owls (or at least in those cultures that do not look upon owls as the embodiment of evil and harbingers of doom). I have only been lucky enough to see just one of the species named in his honour. It was in a wonderful coniferous forest in southern Poland.

We were guided to the old Black Woodpecker hole in a tree that it called home. Our guide then scratched on the tree-trunk in imitation of the sound made by a Pine Martin scrambling up a tree. This evoked the same reaction as the real thing would – the owl popped his head out of the hole like a Jack-in-the-Box to see what was going on. Seeing nothing more dangerous than an admiring tourist or two, he popped back in, out of sight. I am told this is a good way to get such a response wherever arboreal mammals predate birds' eggs.

Birders the world over have found techniques to see birds in ways that are not a threat to them, which either get the birds to come closer to them or become easier to see. The most obvious example is, of course, using a tape lure; that is playing a bird's song or calls that will get a bird of the same species to react to it fearing a predator or rival for territory or mates. This is not fully insulated against harming the bird. If used in the breeding season it can draw birds away from their nestlings or eggs as the parent thinks there is an intruder that must be seen off and can neglect their charges. In the worst case, a bird might see the strong singing rival as too much to cope with and so quits a territory. For this reason this technique is rightly frowned upon during the breeding season or when birds establish territories and even out of such seasons it should be used very sparingly, if at all.

Many birders will also know about 'pishing', although few are completely sure what a 'pish' actually is. This is a technique particularly useful on Autumn migration when many birds will dive deep into bushes in pursuit of fruit rather than their normal insect diet. The 'pish' is a noise made to get the birds pop their heads above the parapet so that you can see what is lurking there when the only evidence you have had so far is a disappearing rump or even just an unidentifiable peep. It is said that birds are investigating the noise because it imitates the contact call of baby birds, but it could as easily be their trepidation, being fearful that the noise emanated from a predator. Pishing can cover everything from a high-pitched sound created by sucking the lips or the back of your hand, to blowing through your clenched teeth while rhythmically moving your lips. It can even be merely saying the word 'pish' breathily and repeatedly in a whisper-like way, sucking in your cheeks and moving your lips.

Round the world I have seen various devices that create similar noises by using a sort of wooden peg that goes into a wooden sleeve dusted with resin powder and then twisting it so that it emits a high-pitched squeak. An alternative, which I adopted and have used to great effect, was shown to me in Australia. You need a small piece of polystyrene of the sort too often used to pack deliveries. You have to wet the glass of your wristwatch (perhaps by licking it) then move the polystyrene rapidly backwards and forwards on the wet glass so that it emits a squeaking that can be irritating and puts your teeth on edge like chalk slipping on a blackboard. I've used this method in Australia and New Zealand and found it excellent in attracting certain birds – Fairywrens, small Honeyeaters, Fantails and Australasian Robins... perhaps because some of their calls are very similar. I suspect some of the sounds made may be too high for human ears to pick up but irresistible to small birds.

I have to say that, having squeaked and pished on several continents, it seems least effective here at home in the UK. It could be that our bird sounds are different or that our general background noise levels are higher than elsewhere. I've not found it effective on Common Warblers, but it certainly works for Gold- and Firecrests, Dunnocks and Robins and some of the warblers that turn up on passage. In North America it seems pretty effective too.

Although I have not seen it, I understand that imitating the call of a certain owl in North America attracts lots of interest from passerines that come to the calls in order to 'mob' the owl. However, I have seen something similar in South Africa. In a spot where there were already quite a variety of passerines we played a tape of a Pearl-spotted Owlet. This attracted a great deal of interest from a variety of birds such as Waxbills and Batis. We spent 20 minutes watching all the birds it called in, and the commotion attracted a 34-strong troupe of Banded Mongooses too! Eventually, a real Pearl Spotted Owlet was attracted, although it did not stay long as it was immediately mobbed!

Not all man-made attractants are audio... there is a technique, which I have used to good effect that brings in nightjars. As soon as you hear churring males, take out a white hanky and begin to flick it into the air, much as you might flick a table napkin to unfold it before dining. This is said to have the same appearance as the white wing-patches under the wings of the males that seem to flicker with each wing beat. Other males come to see what's going on, judging this to be part of the displaying bird's territorial behaviour. It is a great method of attraction but does have one drawback – that of potentially being mistaken for a crazed, all-night Morris Dancer.

Attempts to attract birds can backfire. I read of a case where, every night, a man would imitate the calls of a Tawny Owl and would hear the call returned. This went on for some weeks before he discovered that the respondent was not another owl, but another birder, also imitating Tawny Owl calls in order to attract one!

In the UK no less than 20 million households put out food for garden birds… an amazing act of altruism which has now been going on for many decades. However, some of us are far more manipulative – we birders not only feed the birds because we care for and about them, which we do, but also because we want new and different birds to visit our gardens and wish to get a good look at them. In my case there are at least three motivations, altruism, selfishness (I want to see them) and indolence (I want to see them without even getting off my fat backside to go look for them where they live).

I have a postage stamp garden. I live on a hill, and my garage is set lower than the house, so we managed to almost double the size of the garden by turning the garage roof into a patio! There is no space for trees, but a couple of neighbours do, so I have a tree-sized Pyrocantha hanging over the fence, forming part of my yard. I have a small garden pond with two tiny strips of border where shrubs are long established and the rest was laid to crazy paving when we moved in 14 years ago. I have systematically ripped up some of this in order to plant a few more shrubs and the rest is covered with dozens of pots of varying sizes.

We do like flowers and the colour they bring, but almost everything is planted to attract birds, directly or otherwise. Berry bushes, including evergreen honeysuckle, are good for autumn passage when Blackcaps and Chiffchaffs drop in. The flowering plants attract butterflies, bees and other insects, which no doubt get picked off by birds and certainly add to the 'aerial plankton' that the Swifts find floating above the house.

On the garage there is a crab apple tree with fruits that last through the winter and which we hope, one day, will prove irresistible to a passing flock of Waxwings. I have a couple of grape vines that are methodically stripped by Blackbirds, as are the currants and wild strawberries. Patio pots seem to be quite a good habitat for insects, as Wrens and Robins, Dunnocks and even an occasional overwintering warbler like to pick around them. To Maggie's annoyance, the Blackbirds love to dig out any loose soil in the pots in the hope of finding a worm or two. We still have a neighbourhood Song Thrush that does its best to pick the snails from their hiding places among the pots.

We live in an area with a large and growing population of feral Ring-necked Parakeets. My conservation core knows they should be culled, but my tree-hugging soft outer covering loves them to pieces and so we set out to attract them into the yard. We put apples on strings and suspended them from our feeders and the overhanging bushes. This worked in the end, and it was a joy to watch them sitting on a branch pulling the string up 'hand over hand' and then taking a decent bite out of the fruit. Eventually we suspended this practice because they started to rip our feeders apart. Even the strongest mesh peanut feeders were no match for their wire-cutter beaks.

For years we saw no Goldfinches in our garden but then hit upon the notion of offering them Nyjer seed. After a couple of weeks this attracted birds and now, whether or not we put out Nyjer, we get up to two dozen goldfinches charming the seeds from the feeders and chattering on the telephone cable to my office. Put out fat in any form and the Blue Tits and Great Tits are soon bullied off by a positive horde of Starlings. I planted more Pyrocantha bushes to keep the Blackbirds happy, and this has, on odd occasions, enticed a Redwing into view. Of course, our proverbial trails of breadcrumbs not only attract the birds we want, but the entire local population of Feral Pigeons, as well as the increasing army of Collared Doves. Fat squares put out for the songbirds also pull in a couple of Magpies. Being coastal, the biggest problem is with gulls. A Herring Gull can polish off a lot of goldfish, so we have had to lay canes across the pond that are too flimsy to support the weight of a large gull.

Despite the tiny size and urban location, our back yard hosts huge numbers of birds through the course of a day and a surprising variety over the seasons. Of course, nothing attracts birds as much as other birds, something that duck hunters realised ages ago. I have twice fallen foul (no pun intended) of the practice. Many years ago I spent ages trying to get a good look at what appeared to be a ring on the leg of a roosting Oystercatcher on nearby mudflats. It was not until the tide came in and inundated the 'bird', that I realised it was a model stuck into the ground to attract other waders to be counted. The 'ring' was just some red wire securing the wader to a stake! More recently, on a winter's day watching from a hide at a local reserve, and despite the strong wind, I tried for ages to get a good ID on the duck that was tucked up halfway behind an island on a scrape. I was still watching when another birder joined me in the hide and asked the perennial question 'Anything about?'... as I had responded with the usual 'Not a lot!' he drew my attention to a snipe on the island. At first I couldn't see it until he told me it was about three feet to the left of the decoy... I had spent 20 minutes trying to get the ID of a plastic duck!

Birders the world over have found techniques to see birds in ways that are not a threat to them, which either get the birds to come closer to them or become easier to see. The most obvious example is, of course, using a tape lure; that is playing a bird's song or calls that will get a bird of the same species to react to it fearing a predator or rival for mates or territory.

U is for Ural Owl
(Ural Owl, *Strix uralensis*)

I am sure that Maggie is not alone in favouring owls above all other birds. Owls are somehow mysterious and beautiful, but also seem close to us with their forward looking eyes and frank, blinking gaze. We have seen a good number of species around the world, but mostly roosting during the day. Almost all of the owls we have seen on the move have been at home, with the most frequent sightings being of Barn and Short-eared Owls. Both species are not truly nocturnal and can be seen mornings and evenings quartering lowland marshes in the winter, with Short-eared Owls often seen in the 'simmer din' hunting for voles across plantations and moors in the Scottish Highlands. We have seen a few Barn Owls overseas and caught a glimpse of a few birds taking brief flights elsewhere, but only once have we ever been able to follow another owl species.

In northern Hungary we were slowly driving along a woodland track in search of Woodpeckers, whilst being serenaded by Hawfinches and Semi-collared Flycatchers. We rounded a corner and emerged into a broad area of grass bordered by mature pine trees. From a tree besides us an owl took flight and slowly glided the full length of the clearing as we continued to drive. It rounded a corner and flew on as the grassland gave way to marsh and birch scrub before the forest closed in again. For perhaps 600 yards we had followed the owl in its silent, ghost-like glide through the forest glade hardly taking a breath as if not to break the spell it wove around us. It is easy to see why such beasts are feared in some places as they appear out of nowhere and disappear again without a sound, so that it is hard to know if they are real or imagined.

Of course, the forests themselves seem to hold a magic quality. The trees absorb even natural sounds, and one can imagine that the world outside has disappeared and is now clothed in the wild wood of millennia ago. Indeed, in eastern Europe there are still great tracts of forest hardly exploited or harmed by man that clothe vast areas of land. Nowhere is this more so than in Poland where the Białowieza forest straddles the border with Belarus. This area, said to be the last primeval forest left in Europe, is so vast that during the Second World War a whole army of patriots held out there, and the Nazi invaders could neither tease them out nor overwhelm them. It is still home to Elk and Brown Bear, Wolves, Lynx, European Bison and a host of other fauna either extinct or rare elsewhere. For more than 7,000 years the hand of man has hardly touched parts of the forest, so that there are 4,000 species of fungi, numerous mosses and grasses, and unexpected woodland flowers. Oak, Ash, Lime and Spruce predominate with soaring Hornbeams, which are the perfect habitat for Hawfinches, in its 1,500 square miles.

When Maggie and I visited this forest in early May it was completely carpeted with Wood Anemones and was quite as beautiful as an English Bluebell wood. We were, of course, seeking out its special birds, and, although we did not see any Ural Owls, we did see many other birds, including woodpeckers. After a great deal of effort on the part of a local guide, even I managed to see a European Pygmy Owl. Not only are they quite elusive, but also the 'window' in time is narrow – for just a few minutes in fact, as the sun sets when it is just light enough to see, and you can, with luck, catch sight of one or more of these little beauties. Having a back that barely bends means that I find it very hard to look up into the canopy. This is quite a disadvantage for a birder, so I have learned various tricks and wrinkles to get me into a position where I can see what most people have no trouble with.

Often I carry a small folding stool and plonk myself down on it in order to tip backwards, so my face points upwards. Otherwise I slide my back part way down a tree trunk and bend my knees, giving me a good view up into the trees but also a sore back and creaky knees. In fact, bending my knees in order to look upwards only works for a few minutes, as I have to rest with increasing frequency until my thighs are burning like a rabbit on a spit. The trick is to look up for as little as I can, and I often rely on Maggie to literally give me the 'heads up'.

When birding in tropical forests, where the trails often accommodate vehicles, I use them in various ways to aid my birding. Sometimes I lean back against a bonnet to look upwards, at other times I slide open a door and use a step to sit on and lean back into the cab in order to scan the skies or birdwatch the treetops. On this occasion I was squirming around on the bonnet of the forester's car as he tape-lured the Pygmy Owl to our spot. Each time the bird landed at the top of a Spruce tree, I found the right place to lean back onto the bonnet in such a way as to get my bins pointing at the bird, and each time I managed it the bird lost interest and moved perches.

Seeing my problem, our forester friend motioned to me to stay stretched out on the bonnet of his car, gesturing that I should get into a relatively comfortable position and hold that pose. He then squatted down beside me so that he could see what I could see. He committed to memory the treetops in my view and then abandoned his tape machine, instead imitating the owl calls himself. When the owl returned, the forester moved about still calling, and the bird hopped from treetop to treetop, keeping pace with him. Eventually the owl hove into view for me, and I raised my binoculars for a good long look as the forester stopped imitating calls and instead broadly grinned at me with both his thumbs up!

One of the birds that we (Maggie, my mate Andy, who was the other participant on this trip, and I) most wanted to see was Hazel Hen. They are not a particularly rare bird but they are fairly shy and very cryptic in plumage, so seeing them is not straightforward.

As we drove around the tracks that criss-cross much of the forest, our guide, Bogash, would stop and make Hazel Hen calls. On a couple of occasions the calls were returned. On one such occasion, one flew from one side of the track to the other. However, it was quite high up, and only Bogash who was driving and I who was next to him saw it at first. It was a fleeting glimpse, but it landed on the side of the track that Maggie was on in the back of the car, and she too had the merest of views. In the birding world this is what some of us call 'a tick but not a view'. In other words there was no doubt that we had seen the bird but had it not been identified by the guide and called in by him, we would have had no sighting at all, and what we did get was more frustrating than satisfying.

As far as our companion was concerned this was worse than no sighting. This was because he could not even claim to have caught a movement from the corner of his eye. Now despite around a quarter of a century of denial, Andy does not believe that I am not a competitive birder. He is convinced that I get pleasure from seeing birds that he has not, over and above the pleasure derived from seeing a new bird for my life list. No matter how hard I try to convince him otherwise, his conviction is unshakeable – and it rankles. There were and are, I have no doubts, nights that he is robbed of sleep by thoughts of species I have seen that he has not. It doesn't matter to him that his world- and UK-list are longer than mine, despite him having started birding a generation later than me. Andy is a dyed-in-the-wool lister. To illustrate this, while we were in Africa he tried to get someone to row him across a river just so that he could get an Angola list. Meanwhile, and perhaps pathetically, I was content to start an Angola list based on what I saw on the far bank and could ID with a scope.

Indeed while in Poland we went to the Belarus border to see if they would allow us across. Earlier in the day we had both created a Belarus list by watching a Common Buzzard soaring across the border. However, Andy also keeps a list of the countries he has visited so he wanted to step across the line and get a passport stamp. Although the Polish border guards were happy to oblige, the stone-faced Belarussians were impervious to every plea. So it was that, the next day out in the woods, Andy was determined to claw back the Hazel Hen tick.

Having driven up and down the tracks for a while, we stopped at a very pretty spot of open woodland carpeted with Wood Anemones and other spring flowers. Everywhere were fallen trees hung with moss and areas of young growth. All around was the wonderful spicy smell of woodland. Our guide had overheard a Hazel Hen call, and the four of us wandered about in the wood, always in sight of our car on the track, seeing if we could find the bird, but to no avail.

Andy moved further into the wood, and when the rest of us decided to give up and move on, he was out of sight. We slowly made our way back to the car and waited for him to join us. After nearly half an hour we began to be concerned, knowing that during WW2 German troops had often got lost deep in the wood never to be seen again! We began to call and whistle, but there was no response. After another half an hour we were on the point of leaving for help from the forest authorities when, half a mile down the track, we saw Andy emerge from the woodland, turn around and spot us then nonchalantly light a cigarette. When he walked back to us he seemed completely unconcerned. It was only later that he admitted that he had become completely disoriented and decided that his only safe choice was to just walk in the direction he was facing, never deviating, until he hit a track. It was complete luck that he emerged on the right track and within site of us! Although most of our birding time in the woodland was in managed wood, one can imagine just how dense the forest is where no trees are felled and what falls is left in place.

Białowieza forest is a very special area, a treasure for the whole of Europe, as is the other great bird area in the country, Biebrza marsh. During our late spring visit whole valleys seemed to be a blaze of gold from the huge areas of Marsh Marigold. There are special birds here such as Great Snipe and River Wabler; we staked out sites for both during our visit and were rewarded with brief views of Great Snipe as dusk fell, which even kept up our spirits when we had to dig the car out of the muddy track that we had driven down to get to the site. River Warblers sang for us where marsh gave way to woodland, a song, once heard, never to be forgotten... even by me! Nevertheless, no one species is as impressive as the sheer numbers of some. In the UK I have been lucky enough to see a lek of a dozen Ruff in East Anglia... at one spot in Biebrza we saw more than 1,000 Ruff all in their individual breeding plumage, one of the great sites of the birding world.

...half a mile down the track, we saw Andy emerge from the woodland, turn around and spot us then nonchalantly light a cigarette...

V is for Victorin's Warbler
(Victorin's Warbler, *Cryptillas victorini*)

Victorin's Warbler has a special place in my emotional locker –
I hate it with a vengeance. What, you may ask, has this tiny
Southern African species ever done to deserve such
approbation? Well, it is not so much what it has done, as what
it has not! On my one visit to South Africa I was taken to a
gorge in the Fynbos where this particular species has a home. It
is not common there, in fact, it is far from common anywhere.
We set up our scopes looking down into a rocky gully where
one large bush grew as our guide heard the warbler calling.
Soon we were also hearing its distinct calls. Now the thing
about this warbler is that it is an extremely poor flyer; its wings
are virtually vestigial and it hardly bothers with flight at all,
preferring instead to creep around in low bushes seeking out
food. It was the breeding season, so tape-lures could not be used
or at least not if we wanted to keep our consciences clear. So we
spent an hour or more hoping for a glimpse, all the while
hearing the bird's calls. Our time was very limited as we had
arranged to be elsewhere and, even overstaying by nearly
another hour, we eventually had to give up and move on.

This means that by my rules the bird does make it to my
life list but only as an 'H Only' – that is a bird heard but not
seen. I hate this, not least because the chances of me having
picked out a bird for myself on call alone is diminishingly small.
For most such ticks I have to rely upon the better ears and
audio ID skills of someone else, usually a guide. Moreover, if
the bird lived in Kent I would have plenty of chances to go try
and turn the 'heard only' into a 'proper' tick. But the likelihood

of my returning to South Africa is very slim, unless the European Lottery obliges. That annoying 'H' will likely be there for as long as I keep lists. Unfortunately, it is not alone.

Another very irksome bird is the Maroon-fronted Parrot from south of the border down Mexico way. This is another bird with an extremely limited range. I am aware of only one nesting cliff in Mexico. This is across a wide valley on private land, so the only place to view it is perhaps a mile away on a public road. With a scope this would be possible despite many intervening trees, but in an afternoon spent waiting for one to show, with their annoying calls coming across the valley to us, we never managed to get more than a glimpse of a few birds that 'might have been' which were gone before our optics swung into position. Several of us sat waiting away the hours in strained hope rather than firm expectation. It was at the hottest part of the day and nothing much else was about. The only other bird we saw was an Acorn Woodpecker and even it had got bored, climbed to the top of a power pole and, as we were in danger of, nodded off! Once again, I very much doubt that I will return to this isolated spot. There it sits on my list, an 'H' burning its way like a fire worm into my memory, taunting me.

Unfortunately, this situation is likely to worsen. As I become less and less able to hike along jungle trails, more and more species become likely to elude me. On a trip to Panama in recent years there were several birds whose calls I heard repeatedly without seeing the caller. For the most part, these were types of Antbird, such as the Orange-billed Nightingale Thrush, that stick to the leaf litter and follow ant swarms around while they try and pick off the insects or arachnids and so forth that army ants scare into the open. I heard this bird on several occasions at different sites and, despite carefully waiting in ambush, never managed even a glimpse of it. On another occasion a guide brought my attention to the call of a Grey-breasted Woodhen. He pointed to where the noise came from and I watched the progress of the bird as it moved aside the undergrowth, but I never actually saw the bird!

In Sri Lanka it was the Brown-capped Babbler. We crept through a small wood as the bird called, then crept back through the same wood as it still called, but whichever way we walked it was always moving away from us. We chased this fine fellow three times in three different localities but it never showed its face!

My most recent heard-only ticks were on a trip to Jamaica and Cuba. While with guides, we heard but did not see the Rufous Mourner in Jamaica. I also got very used to the mournful call of the Sad Flycatcher. However, it remained out of site to me on every occasion, although my old mate Andy managed a view and could barely keep the grin off his face – despite his words of consolation. But the worst 'cryptic species' by far was the Yellow-shouldered Grassquit. We heard several birds call on two occasions while with guides, then heard them again (the birds not the guides) a few feet from the entrance to our hotel. This was worst partly because my oldest birding friend and rival saw the birds, called our attention to them and pointed out the call as we searched a vegetable patch for one to re-appear. They were mixed with another species of grassquit and other birds, so I stood there in dying light, swinging my bins up to every movement, while being eaten alive by vicious mosquitos and yet I still managed to dip out. I fear that there is now no way that I'll be able get back there to turn the 'H' into a 'proper' tick!

Sometimes things seem to conspire to rob one of the visual contact that you most crave. In Cuba, down near the Zapata Swamps, we were told where a flock of Cuban Parakeets were seen every night. On our first foray we heard the flock in an orchard, but they moved away before we could see them. On several evenings we returned to the spot but did not connect. Then, on our last chance to see them, I was 'discommoded' by a local bug and had to stay in my quarters, while my fellow travellers went and connected with the birds!

For many years I heard what I presumed to have been Ring Ouzel calls echoing down Scottish glens but, having no faith in my audio skills I never even tempted the birding gods with an 'H'. Had I, the situation may well have remained that way for years while I sought out this particular 'bogey bird'.

In my twitchiest years I was living in Buckinghamshire close to Wendover Woods, which was a known stronghold for breeding Firecrests. Over the course of several seasons I would pitch up at a specially built hide hoping to see them. (Often the sting of disappointment was somewhat soothed by great views of Crossbills which were regular visitors and often easy to see in large numbers in the hand clearings amongst the mature pines). For a couple of years I never even heard the little blighters, partly because their songs are quiet and very high pitched. On one occasion I did manage to hear some, although they remained hidden high overhead. Eventually I caught up with them during their autumn passages, many miles from Wendover, and that was after seeing them overseas where they are far more common.

Turning an 'H' to a full tick is something I would try to do if an opportunity arose. On the few times I've managed it, it seems to be the height of good fortune and gives a feeling of satisfaction like no other. The most satisfying occasion was turning Quail from heard to seen as it was the longest standing bogey bird, having literally been an 'H only' for many years.

The annoying 'H' had lasted years despite being repeated in the UK most years, but the conversion happened on the side of a road in South Africa. It was some years after that, that the only 'H' on my British list was erased when I came upon a family group of quail caught out in the open in my home county. The worst to bear remains the pardalote (see p. 155), as I have had several bites at this cherry. Who knows when, or even if, I will get back to Australia to search for it once more.

Similarly, half an hour spent circling the same small patch of trees at a hotel in The Gambia, hearing Oriole Warbler calling constantly, was another major frustration that I hope to put right one day. Yet, only the birding gods surely know whether I will ever return to West Africa.

Half an hour spent circling the same small patch of trees at a hotel in The Gambia hearing Oriole Warbler calling constantly was another major frustration that I hope to put right one day, but only the birding gods know whether I will ever return to West Africa.

W is for Wallcreeper
(Wallcreeper, *Tichodroma muraria*)

I have known of the Wallcreeper since early childhood because it was portrayed on a   small illustrated cards, so-called cigarette cards, found in packets of tea in the 1950s; these cards were in effect the successor of small collectable cards which were originally included in packets of cigarettes. However, by the 1950s, there were no more cigarette cards as such, the only inserts in 'fags' then were gift vouchers... 'Embassy' and 'No 6' were two brands that gave you coupons to collect while you smoked... the joke at the time was that you could save them up to get your own iron lung! Collectable cards were then to be found only in packets of tea... loose tea, as teabags had not yet become popular. Brooke Bond Tea was our household favourite, and they produced some excellent series of cards such as British Birds. So, ever since seeing a picture of the Wallcreeper, I had longed to see this crimson and grey marvel for real. In my youth I assumed they were to be found on the walls of local castles and the like and I was not disabused of this belief until taking up 'proper' birding in my late teenage years. It was then that the myth was snatched from me when I found out that they were rare even 'on the Continent'. The dream of seeing one became a strong desire that remained with me and I even visited a couple of places where they could, with great luck, be found... but my luck was not so great on those occasions.

Wallcreeper would be a 'wanted' tick for many people because it is a family all by itself – see one and you cannot only tick a species but cross off an entire family of birds from the 'needed' list. For me, though, it was the unlikely combination of Battleship Grey and Vermillion feathers that drew me to it. Observed only from behind it could hide against the walls of a canyon and be nearly impossible to see until it flashed colour by stretching out those wings with the contrasting white and vermillion flashes. Sitting still, the red that shows on the wing could be mistaken for mineral staining on a rock face, but in action nothing about the bird can be mistaken for anything else but this rare delight.

This was not, and is not, the only iconic bird I have long wanted to see, but it is, perhaps, the one I longed for longest... and the day I finally made its acquaintance in the flesh is one of those memories which will remain long after I have forgotten what day of the week it is or my own name! When I saw it at last it was unexpected, unlooked for and almost overlooked but eventually overwhelming.

I knew that northern India held Wallcreepers and had even kept my eyes open as we travelled up from Delhi to Corbett National Park. But once inside this wonderful area of forest and clearings I was after other targets more obviously found in that habitat.

On our first day in the park we searched a trail for the rather elusive Jungle Fowl which half the party (in the lead vehicle) managed to find and some of us managed to miss. Eventually, a bird was obliging enough to run back into the shrubbery right past our 'Gypsy', so that we had short but excellent views. This meant that we could move on to other targets. Over the river there was a place where we could watch for Maroon Orioles, so we headed for that spot. To get there we had to cross a very wide, but also very shallow, river. Before descending the bank, we approached very cautiously because of a local elephant. Apparently there is one very territorial chap which doesn't like interlopers and charges other pachyderms. Those on safari need to be vigilant, too, as he has decided that any vehicle is an honorary elephant and he has been known to turn over a jeep!

The trick is to creep up to the bank, checking whether he is about or not, then putting the pedal to the metal until clear of the trees and onto the flat gravel river bed. The drivers did just this and weaved their way between some massive, house-sized boulders, only slowing down when we reached the halfway point that seemed clear of musk-maddened tuskers. As we came to a virtual standstill close to one of the giant boulders, a bird suddenly quit the crevice it was clinging to and flashed by us before slapping into to another jumbo boulder and sticking to it.

There it was, the lifer I had waited half a lifetime to see. Tears sprang to my eyes unexpectedly and embarrassingly, as I punched the air triumphantly. Then I sat back when the most sudden and excruciating headache hit me between the eyes. It is what I would describe as an 'ice-cream headache', the sort that follows what Americans call 'brain freeze'. It lasted the rest of the day but was nothing compared to the exaltation. I felt an elephantine euphoria, as my longest standing avian wish was fulfilled.

Maybe it is my age, but I find that when such birding dreams do come true my emotions bubble up to the surface and burst out for all to see; but making a complete prat of myself seems a small price to pay for the brilliance of those beautiful birding jewels.

In Botswana one boat ride included two longed-for moments! Roosting in a Jacaranda tree hanging above the river was a Pel's Fishing Owl – another bird seen on an old cigarette card sometime in my youth. It had moved to the fore during my research for *Whose Bird*, which created another ambition, to see examples of any bird named after someone. (Pel was the Dutch Governor of Ghana from 1840 to 1850 and was an amateur naturalist.) The other bird was a more short-term desire – more than a decade before I had been to The Gambia but did not connect with a very colourful bird – the Carmine Bee-eater, and had wanted to ever since. When we drifted up to where over 100 pairs nested in holes in the clay bank I was again rather emotionally overwhelmed. Not just to see the bird, but to have dozens within touching distance was an ambition fulfilled beyond dreams! There should be a word that describes the opposite of 'dipping out', when your long-held wish is fulfilled.

In South Africa we had a wonderful last minute tick that compensated for my long-regretted lack of a Moroccan list in general and Bald Ibis in particular. My holiday in Morocco was during my salad days when lazing in the sun with my female companion was further up the list of worthy pursuits than looking for birds. I don't recall seeing any birds there at all, which illustrates just how deep I had sunk into my avian despond. Only afterwards did I realise that one of the world's iconic species has its dwindling presence mostly in that country... the Bald Ibis. Despite the fact that, like Carmine Bee-eater, the species was split into its northern and southern varieties, I would have been happy to settle for either. So when we were being driven back to the airport in Johannesburg for our journey home I was less interested in being told by our driver that the airport had, between the time of our landing and departure, been renamed Oliver Tambo Airport, than in what else he had to say, namely 'Look out for Southern Bald Ibis, as they have been seen along this road.' Maggie had the presence of mind to ask what they looked like and, as he finished giving a description, she said: 'Like the birds we just passed, you mean?' In common with far too many bird guides John looked askance as his chauvinism seemed to be winning over his experience (having seen Maggie spot birds on the trip that no one else even noticed). 'Are you sure?' he asked, reluctantly pulling over to the verge. 'Do you want me to turn around?'

Everyone else in the vehicle insisted, as they all knew that 'Hawkeye' was seldom wrong. John turned back and we all started searching the rolling hills until Maggie pointed to the group of three Southern Bald Ibis picking their way through a field right next to the road!

When I first started birding there was another iconic species that I wanted to see simply because it looked so exotic and yet did sometimes turn up in the UK – the Hoopoe. In my early twitching days, I dipped out on the species enough for it to be even higher on my list of 'please let me see one'… a wheedling plea to the gods of birding. Eventually Maggie and I did catch up with one and at first glance it was smaller and less conspicuous than we had imagined. Having seen a few on such twitches it was not until our first overseas birding forays that it did justice to our earlier fantasies. This is a bird that must be seen in flight as its chequerboard wings make it look like a giant butterfly. Moreover, to see a pair in courtship on a dusty Iberian road raising its crest in agitation or excitement is always an amazing sight. It was long wished for and whenever seen doesn't disappoint. It is one of the joys of holidaying in southern Europe to sit on your balcony on a summer evening, maybe with bee-eaters hawking around you and hear the 'ooo ooo' call of a hoopoe echoing across a valley.

Of course, keen birders will recognise that the 'long wished for' species, if it seems eminently obtainable but remains elusive, can become a nemesis or 'bogey bird'. Often this will stick with one for years to come for no obvious reason.

I used to have two UK bogey birds… Ring Ouzel (see D) and Cirl Bunting. The latter has a very restricted range in the headlands of the south-west, so I had an excuse. These days it is still on the list, but once I had seen the species overseas I could not justify chasing it too hard, and life rarely takes me to that part of the world these days. If and when it does I will put a bit of effort into seeking one out, especially as, through the hard work of local farmers and conservationists, their numbers have begun to build up in suitable habitat.

My excuse with the Ring Ouzel was its breeding habitat – high moorlands. They have never been a numerous bird as potential homes are scarce here, and in the last few years numbers have declined, even where suitable habitat has been conserved. For most of my adult life, because I have had some restriction as to the distance I can walk, the task of finding them where they live during the summer has always been difficult and has mostly proved beyond me. However, they do pass right through the area where I live during spring and autumn passage. In spring, given the right weather conditions, they will land on the local clifftops and marshes. Indeed, these days I consider it a poor spring when I do not connect with one.

In the autumn in coastal areas where there are fruiting bushes that attract them, the birds can fatten up for the long flight south. Most autumns I will now see a few picking their way along the hedgerows, like Blackbirds with silvery wings. Yet, I was well past my twitching years before I finally saw my first one on the most unexpected of places. I was walking through a little patch of woodland at Minsmere in Suffolk, looking for tits and tree-creepers and other typical woodland species when a Ring Ouzel landed in a small clearing in front of me. It was such a shock that I nearly ruined the sighting by dropping my binoculars and frightening it away but managed to keep hold of them, as well as my composure, and hold my breath too.

There have been other lesser moments, impressions of which still stay with me, of birding wishes fulfilled… not to mention many more anticipated. The one which left the greatest impression was not even a wish of my own. The deep impression was left on my leg when Maggie fulfilled her earliest birding ambition – that of seeing a Green Woodpecker for the first time – she did not punch the air, but chose instead to punch my thigh so hard that I could not walk for half an hour after!

The drivers weaved their way between some massive, house-sized boulders only slowing as we reached the halfway point that seemed clear of musth maddened tuskers. As we came to a virtual standstill close to one of the giant boulders, a bird suddenly quit the crevice it was clinging to and flashed by us before slapping into to another jumbo boulder and sticking to it.

X is for Xenops
(Plain Xenops, *Xenops minutus*)

The Plain Xenops is ostensibly, as the name suggests, a rather dull fellow. It is a member of an interesting family, the Furnariidae, otherwise known as the Ovenbirds; they create elaborate kiln-like nests from clay. The Plain Xenops is, however, also the 'plain Jane' of nest builders, merely shredding a little plant material to line a hole in a tree. Its song is also an unremarkable 'fit fit fit f ff f'. Many of the family have delightful sage-green or light-blue eggs... not so our poor plain birds; theirs are white as driven snow. In the lowland forests of Panama (where I have seen several Plain Xenops) they are hard to see as they forage for insects, blending into the leaf-litter or against a plain brown log as they search for, appropriate enough, boring beetles. In other words, there really is nothing outstanding about these birds apart, of course from their name, odd on the eye and hard to pronounce.

It is pronounced ZENN-ops. The only reason it is not spelt with a 'Z' is that the scientific name was coined first and the 'common' name is the same, because this sadly unremarkable bird inspired no other in those who discovered, collected and studied it. Most scientific names are created from Latin or Greek. In this case *Xen'os* is Ancient Greek for 'strange' or, perhaps, 'foreign'... so this clearly normal – nay boring – bird is, apparently, strange!

The pronouncing of bird names is nowhere near as obvious as I have always assumed it to be. I was hearing, only recently, about the last ditch attempt to save a Madagascan duck from the very brink of extinction. There were as few as 30 individuals in the wild, so some have been taken into care and are producing chicks that are now being reintroduced into their normal habitat. They are a species of pochard. I have always called such ducks *potch*-ard as in *notch*, but one reporter described them as *poach*-ard.

The next day I heard the same pronunciation in the question on a TV quiz. A new one on me, but I have come across many differences in the pronunciation used by birders, particularly, but not exclusively, between different countries. Moreover, there is an on-going controversy as to the 'proper' plurals of whole groups of birds. Native English speakers tend to use the singular form when talking in the plural for whole families. In England *most* birders refer to several waders, ducks, pheasants and grouse, among other families, exactly as they refer to one individual. That is to say, most of us would say three grouse, four snipe, nine pintail and so forth. On the other hand, we would say there are seven swans, three geese and a couple of partridges?

There is no logic to this as it is a matter of convention rather than grammar. Non-native English speakers tend to use the 'correct' plural, such as six snipes, two teals and a dozen woodcocks. Even these conventions are not consistent. In the UK one can say three Greylag or three Greylags, and both sound right! Nor is there complete consensus even among, say, English birders some of whom use singular names and some plurals when there are more than one mallard or bean goose. This is further complicated by a tendency to try and 'pluralise' part of a name that should not be changed. It would be correct to say there are several Pinkfooted Geese, but most of us would say there are several Pinkfeet! Just think how we all panic if required to comment upon more than one Mongoose!

Even more recently, another lack of consensus became apparent as I tried (unsuccessfully unlike my darling wife) to twitch a local Hoopoe. I have always said 'Hoop-poh' whereas many say 'Hoo-Poo'. As the name is onomatopoeic perhaps I am in the wrong here as the bird definitely calls 'hoo poo poo poo'!

In some cases I have been really thrown by a bird name being pronounced very differently without me even considering that there is more than one way to do it. When we birded in Southern Africa our guide pointed out a species of plover to us… saying pl-*over* as in the word 'over' (I gather this is also the preferred pronunciation in the US), whereas I have always said, and always heard it pronounced, as *pluvver* as in the word 'lover'. I was also recently taken aback when someone asked me at a winter watchpoint, if there were any 'Woo-per' swans about and I replied that, as far as I knew, no one had seen any 'Hooper' swans. The dictionary allows for both, although, I am sure, the majority in the UK would go with me on this one. It does seem that most people pronounce 'whoop' as woop and say 'wooping cough', whereas I say 'hoop' and 'hooping coff'!

There are two birds, which being foreign, I definitely mispronounced on first seeing them. Both occur in Australia, and in one case someone corrected me when I said: 'Jeri-gon' rather than 'ger-RIG-on'ee' when confronted with a Gerygone. I learnt the correct way to pronounce the other species in South Africa where I was told by a Guide that it was easy to remember how to pronounce Cisticola correctly rather than saying, as I had, 'sisty-CO-la. He said it was easy to remember to say 'siss-TIC-ola' as it rhymed with 'pep-SIC-ola', which I thought a neat joke.

Pronunciation is, of course, not even half of the problem. There is no consensus, despite a number of attempts, to standardise common names. Indeed, not even scientific names are universal, sometimes through disagreement on taxonomic status, other times purely as different nations choose to use different species or even family names for the same bird! When everyone agreed that the Eurasian Great White Egret and the North American Great Egret were one and the same bird, the former was called *Egretta alba*, the latter *Casmerodius alba*! Often birds were independently described and, despite the chronologically first description always taking precedence, it is sometimes hard to give up a name that has already been used, especially if that is over a long period.

The move to standardise has only really just begun in earnest because, for the first time, there is a definitive way to be sure about whether a species is new, a sub-species or lesser taxa, or just a mistake. Now, with the aid of DNA sequencing all birds in collections around the world are being 'bar-coded', involving the mitochondrial COI (Cytochrome oxidase I) gene. When this is complete there will, no doubt, still be wrangles over which scientific name to use, although with agreed rules I expect that this will eventually be resolved. At that point we will, at least, know how many species and sub-species have been discovered... possibly?

However, with common names I do not expect there to be a consensus – ever. English common names may be different in England, the US, Southern Africa, Australasia and India! Even when progress is made and some people give up 'their' common name, birders will probably go on using the name they always have. A generation ago there was a move to standardise, often using a geographical tag for, say, American Robin and European Robin... but the Europeans, rightly in my chauvinistic opinion, declared that as historically, a Robin or a Wren have been known as such for centuries there was no need to add 'European', and certainly no need to adopt the American nomenclature of 'Winter Wren' – because we have just the one species all year round. Anyway, some names are just plain wrong, the American Robin isn't a Robin at all… it's really a thrush!

Of course it is pronounced ZENN-ops. The only reason it is not spelt with a 'Z' is that the scientific name was coined first and the 'common' name is the same, because this sadly unremarkable bird inspired no other in those who discovered, collected and studied it. Most scientific names are created from Latin or Greek. In this case Xen'os *is Ancient Greek for 'strange' or, perhaps, 'foreign'... so this clearly normal, nay boring, bird is apparently strange!*

Y is for Yellow-crowned Bishop
(Yellow-crowned Bishop, *Euplectes afer*)

Yellow-crowned Bishops look like huge bumblebees when the males fly during the mating season; they have a peculiar upright position during their upward flights from cover, which are intended to attract females and intimidate other males. I remember seeing my first when we stopped on the side of a road in Kenya's rice growing area. I assume this to be a marshy area where some land had been partially drained to make it suitable for cultivating rice as there were large cultivated areas. These were, when we visited, still reed-fringed and lush with water birds and those birds that like a wetland habitat's edges. Looking through our telescopes to see the birds attracted the interest of some passing youngsters who were clearly confused by what we were doing. Birding is, for the most part, something that people from richer developed countries do, as only they have the leisure time and income to be able to indulge such a pleasurable waste of time.

Naturally, we invited the boys to take a look through our scopes at what we were looking at. Seeing their reaction was fascinating as, on first looking through they jumped back, suddenly surprised by the size of what they were used to seeing from afar. The second reaction, which they all showed, was the confusion with size and proximity. To a boy they all, having got over their initial shock, waved their hands about just in front of them while still viewing, presumably because everything seemed, through a scope, to be brought close enough to touch. Their final reaction was typical of youngsters everywhere, broad grins and laughter at the delight of magnification.

On the one hand this sort of reaction is charming, but on the other it shows how unevenly the distribution of wealth is across the world and particularly in Africa. Where people struggle to make a living, conservation is rarely at the forefront of their minds, and this reinforces that we in the richer nations should be doing all we can to help. 'Green' tourism is only a good thing if it does more good than harm; part of the good that it can do is bring money into poorer countries. It is a wonderful thing that migration means that at least half of 'our' birds spend parts of their lives elsewhere. Thus, to help conserve them and their habitat, we have to look outwards. BirdLife International partners do just that. For example, the RSPB has projects all over the world. People are trained and educated to help too, but if the future of birds is to be assured then those of us who enjoy birding abroad should be doing all we can to make the pursuit pay for the places we travel to. I am a great believer in local people, using locally owned facilities, making all the ground arrangements for groups. It is no good if our birding Pounds, Dollars and Euros just end up in the already packed pockets of multi-national hotel chains and the like.

On another occasion in Kenya, we pulled over to the roadside simply to take a break. As we stretched our legs we could see two or three youngsters looking at us from several fields away. Then a couple of the kids, overcome by the curious sight of a busload of white people strutting about in the midday sun, began to run towards us. After a short while most gave up, but one chap of maybe eight or nine years of age kept coming. He ran like an Olympian barefoot across the crops dodging bushes and avoiding the food plants until he skidded to a halt in front of us. Having reached his goal, he suddenly lost all confidence when Maggie beckoned him over. His eyes went down to his feet; perhaps he had a sudden fear that we were not harmless tourists but might snatch him away. But his curiosity triumphed, and he edged forward. Maggie went through her pockets, and mine, and pulled together all our coins pressing it into the boy's hand. He looked at the pile of coins and his eyes widened; what was inconsequential to us was probably a small fortune to him. He looked up and his face transformed into the widest grin imaginable, and he screwed his hand up tight and began the long run back across the fields.

It is hard not to reward such energetic enterprise and, harder still, not to be moved by the contrast between our lucky lives and those of poor village children. In a rural economy like this you eat what you grow, and harsh and arid weather doesn't just ruin your holiday, but really can mean life or death.

In The Gambia when we drove through small villages we often saw crocodiles of children trailing alongside the vehicle chanting 'toobab, toobab'. This is said to be a corruption of 'two bob', which must have been the price of something in colonial times and now seems to be chanted to white people whenever they are seen. We had been told, when we were planning the trip, to take pens with us, as these are easy to transport and good news for local children where there is no free education, and it's a daily struggle just to get to a classroom, let alone afford writing materials. Despite coming well equipped, we quickly ran out of pens to distribute. We had also brought with us a case-load of new T-shirts and a couple of Chambers Dictionaries to pass on to a local school. Such 'charity' doesn't sit well on the shoulders of a lifelong socialist, but it sits better than ignoring everyone around you. What is so striking in many African countries is that well turned-out, immaculately clean school children emerge every day, from the poorest of homes, to walk miles to school. Keeping our clothes and ourselves clean was hard work even with all the resources of an air-conditioned hotel. The hard work involved in making sure your kids are immaculate from a one-roomed home with a rammed earth floor, and no running water, beggars belief.

In Namibia's Caprivi Strip we left our hotel early to see some of the wonderful birds the area attracts. As we neared our first planned stop, the road was lined for miles with kids on their way to a very nice, newly built secondary school. Some, we worked out as we drove by, had to walk about nine miles in each direction to get there. We turned off the main road down a dirt track to an area of cultivated plots and a tiny mud hut hamlet alongside some sort of orchard. A mile from the road we stopped the vehicle to get out and look at birds in the trees. A few minutes later a girl who was maybe ten years old came over to see what we were doing. In the usual way we showed her what we were doing and let her look through some binoculars. Ready to move on we got back in the vehicle, but before leaving we gave her a bottle of soft drink. We drove off but, looking back, saw her trotting along the track behind us. At our second stop, maybe half a mile further on, she soon caught us up, trailing what we took to be her six-year-old brother. She pushed him forward so that he could take a look through our bins and grin in response. Before moving on again, we found a drink for him, too.

This was repeated with every move until we had finished with this track and turned to leave. By this time we had accumulated an entourage of half a dozen young children all wearing the poorest rags and clutching their empty plastic pop bottles as if they were treasure. We had exhausted all our drinks, lunch packs and small change by the time they waved us off to the main road. Never in rural areas has anyone asked us for anything, poor as they are, merely the chance to satisfy curiosity. Their lives, by our standards, are very poor and certainly hard, but at every age they know that their only way up is by hard work at home, in the fields or at school. I recall driving around an area where we tourists were not allowed out of our vehicles, because of dangerous wild animals, seeing a child of about ten years old herding goats dressed in shorts and a cloak with no more substantial a weapon than a stick.

In India there is a huge difference between town and country. One of our earliest experiences of overseas birding was in Goa. We self-guided there and used old trip reports to find the best places. The most cost effective way of getting around was to hire a taxi by the day. Frankly, driving yourself is a non-starter. Apart from the potholes and madly overcrowded main roads, Goa has a unique heritage of east and west. It was colonised by the Portuguese and if anyone has ever driven in that country they will know that the Portuguese drivers are uniquely macho. Poodle along a quiet road, at a reasonable pace, with half a mile of the road visible ahead and the driver behind will quietly sit on your tail. Speed up and the driver will wait until there is a blind bend at the crest of a hill and will then try to pass; it is as if there is no kudos in merely overtaking, one must wait until it is a challenge and the likelihood of a fatal accident is odds on. Of course, the native people in Goa have several thousand years of fatalism behind them. Combine this with the Portuguese driving heritage and you have a highway code based on prayer and daring. After several days of using the same cab, the driver wanted to make our stay even better and said that he knew of a really good place for birds near his uncle's village. At first we just nodded in a non-committal way, believing that he wanted to please us, and that, not being a birder, he probably meant that there were lots of farmyard geese there. We eventually gave in to his constant assurances and agreed to a trip at the very next daybreak. So it was that we found ourselves by the side of a muddy pool below a steep, wooded hill. The pool, trees and sky were alive with birds, and we clocked up our first Stork-billed Kingfisher, a wonderful Painted Snipe and a very unexpected and rare Lesser-spotted Eagle overhead.

We went on adding new species to our list for an hour or so and then decided to walk around to the other end of the pool for a closer look at the Painted Snipe which picked through the mud churned up by cattle that drank from the pool. So we found ourselves peering through scopes at the muddy pool at the edge of a field. I felt a presence and looked up. There behind me was a queue of children and their parents all waiting for a turn at my scope. No words were exchanged as each took their turn, marvelled at the view through the lenses then bowed politely with hands pressed together as if in prayer to thank me for the experience. They spoke no English, and we spoke no other tongue, so all exchanges were gesture and smiles. As the queue dispersed into the fields, we retired to the one chair café in the village to sip cold Limca (a brand of iridescent bitter lemon pop that probably contains more prohibited colouring and preservative agents than natural ingredients). Despite being in a dirt-poor village by ourselves and carrying several thousands of pounds worth of optical gear round our necks, I felt safer than I would have in broad daylight at a park back home.

In the local town polite curiosity gives way to bustle and begging. We went to a local market and hardly bought anything as our tourist Rupees were very soon maxed out in donations. Maybe there are birders who can resist the large pleading eyes of a nine-year-old girl carrying her four-year-old brother on her back, silently offering a very used plastic bag for sale so as not to be whipped for begging, but not these birders. The same hands held in silent supplication that showed gratitude for a go at our scopes, thanked us for the few Rupees that meant nothing to us but would probably mean a meal for these parentless siblings.

Cities have a very different scale. You are not just met by bustle and begging there, but by pushing and pandemonium. When in Delhi, on another trip, we had been taken into a rather up-market mall to buy souvenirs. Waiting outside its gates for the rest of our group to assemble, one of our number made the mistake of giving a child some sweets that we have been handed on our flight. Within seconds three or four youngsters were pleading for some too, within a minute 20 children were jostling our friend, the sweetie bag had been torn from her hand and the pavement was spread with kids scrapping over the droppings. By the time our guide plucked us from the street and into a vehicle, maybe 30 children were at the scene and another couple of dozen racing to see what was going on. There was no animosity, nor deliberate harm done, just a throng of desperately poor street children trying to survive.

The advice for the green tourist is to 'take nothing but photographs, leave nothing but footprints'. I think we should all add a bit more to this and make our impact positive not neutral; we should all do more than hand out small change to beggars. A donation to a conservation charity is all well and good for those of us who enjoy the wild world, but we should surely also try and make a contribution to the countries we visit that increases the life chances and quality of life of the inhabitants too.

I felt a presence and looked up. There behind me was a queue of children and their parents all waiting for a turn at my scope.

Z is for Zebra Finch
(Zebra Finch, *Taeniopygia guttata*)

Have you ever in your adult life worn wet knickers for three consecutive days? I have, and I blame my wife – if only she had made me listen! This is how it all came about...

When we left New Zealand, after my wife's first visit there, we flew into Sydney en route to the north of Western Australia. Our first onward hop of many hours was to be Perth and, as I had booked our luggage right through to our final destination, I filtered out the tannoy announcement. A confident Australian voice stated that international passengers taking internal flights onward should pick up their luggage and then check it in to their next flight. Maggie had heard this and drew the gist of it to my attention. Typical woman! She would not leave it alone and kept nagging me and pleading that I should go deal with the luggage. But I very reasonably pointed out that there really was no need as I had checked it in at Auckland airport with Qantas, and they had told me it would go right through to Broome, so there were 'no worries'. As fellow long-suffering men will know, this sort of thing happens all too often. I am a seasoned traveller; I've been round the world at least four times, so I know what I am doing. It was all I could do to hold my tongue and keep my temper.

The five-hour flight passed without incident, just lots of boredom and half watched bland films, then we landed in Perth. As I left the plane I double checked with a stewardess and was reassured that our bags would go straight on to the next flight. We barely had time to change planes; the next flight was on a much smaller jet to somewhere I had never heard of – Porthedland. This plane disgorged us into a bijoux airport with a blessedly air-conditioned waiting room, where we paused to take breath and ready ourselves for the last leg to Broome.

There was only a half-hour gap before getting the last flight. This was quite a pleasant break as the waiting room was built around a tiny garden with a tropical shrub growing up in what looked like a roofless glass cage; a really nice glass-walled 'garden' where the wild world could come and go. It also held a very long thin lizard along with a Zebra Finch... that was looking, sadly, just as I have often seen them through a pet shop window. We duly ticked another lifer 'Zebra Finch' before getting on to the 20-seater jet for the last hop.

Thereafter, we soon boarded the next plane – a propeller-driven 10-seater – for the last leg to Broome, idly thinking about all its mouth-watering birding possibilities – several million waders and all those honeyeaters and gerygones. (Here I made the mistake in pronunciation when I told the Australian who was showing me around that I just saw my first 'Gerry gone'. He managed to conceal most of his mirth as he explained to me what the correct pronunciation was – see X).

Broome was a revelation... someone must have left the bath running, as the airport practically steamed with humidity... just the short walk from the plane to the arrivals lounge left us with clothes sticking to our skin. There were just four other passengers with us as we trailed across the baking tarmac to the arrivals hall. Here the sight of the smallest luggage 'carrousel' that I have ever seen greeted us. Eventually a small Australian struggled to the end of the conveyer belt and threw two suitcase on it, which an Australian couple retrieved after it had travelled to the very end – all of six feet away!

A few minutes later he was back with two more bags, which he heaved on to the conveyor – the other Australian couple heaved them off three seconds later. The small porter wiped his brow and took a breather and wished us 'good day'. He walked off in the wrong direction, and Maggie and I looked at each other. A short while later, as a small light bulb clicked on in my mind, I saw an easy-to-interpret look on my beloved's face, accompanied by the sound of the steam escaping from her ears. To be fair, 'she who should always be heeded' merely cocked one eyebrow, while I let my head hang even lower than usual! I looked, unsuccessfully, for somewhere to hide. To give Maggie her due, she just looked skyward, shook her head and then looked down to the floor – but I could hear her softly counting to ten. I guiltily looked around for help. I spotted a tooth-filled fixed smile behind which was the face of the man at the Qantas desk and hurried over to it – I explained to him how I had been let down by my wife's lack of tenacity in the face of my obdurate nature and asked Qantas to locate the bags… 'No worries mate' came the reply as he wandered off to make a call. Ten minutes later he was back. 'No worries mate,' he iterated, 'the bags aren't on the plane.' That much, as I patiently explained, I had managed to work out for myself. 'No worries mate,' he insisted through his porcelain smile. 'I'll go and find out where they are.' He left again, while I marvelled at how quickly he had caught on. Ten further soggy, un-air-conditioned minutes later, he was back. 'They're not in Perth mate,' he informed us (Maggie had joined me, although she was still steaming and emitting deadly penetrating looks) and followed this up with 'No worries mate, we've tracked them down to Sydney and they will go on a plane to Perth as soon as possible – should be here in a day or two.' I thanked him as calmly as I could and explained that we were standing in all the clothes we had with us – just what were we supposed to wear in the meantime? 'No worries mate,' he offered once more. 'We have a totally complimentary Qantas pack here for each of you.

It will give you the necessary toiletries and clothes until yours arrive, free of charge of course, so, er, well, er no worries mate!'

It was at this point that I politely informed him that indeed I did have worries, that I was not his mate, and, should he care to use either phrase again, I would help him into a similar state of worry, involving countless contusions and considerable damage to his porcelain dental work. He gave us a number to call, to check on progress of our baggage the next day, and told us that the airport was now closing, as no more flights were due in or out that day. He took the precaution of closing the shutters before I could remonstrate further and then began turning out the lights in the arrivals hall, while we groped our way to the exit.

Before leaving the UK we had arranged to be shown birds in the Broome area by an ex-pat British guide. He had told us that he would pick us up from the airport bar an hour after our flight came in, so we took our newly acquired Qantas emergency kits to the bar and took a look around. I bought a beer to cool my nerves, temper and body and an ice-cold diet coke for Maggie, hoping that this deed would have the same effect on her, then we took a look at the Qantas' 'goody bag'. Inside each pack was a tiny bar of soap, a razor, a tiny toothbrush and miniature tube of toothpaste wrapped up in a pair of shorts and a T-shirt.

Holding up the T-shirt, it became apparent that Qantas believed all their passengers to be anorexic elves. Had I been able to get the T-shirt over my head it would have barely have become a self-respecting cravat. The shorts might have made a handy duster had they been more generous with the thin cotton material – I doubted whether even the most anorexic elf would have worn them as, even without stretching, they would have been as embarrassingly revealing as a French cyclist's Speedos!

A few minutes later we were explaining all this to George when he met us in the airport bar. Our guide had duly arrived, had a beer, and we discussed the next day's birding. It was agreed that George would pick me up at first light, while Maggie would try and sleep herself into this new time zone. He assured me that I would be OK as the 4x4 was fully air-conditioned and we would see plenty of great birds to take my mind off our woes. He then thoughtfully took charge of the phone number we had been given and promised that he would chase our luggage until it was delivered to us. This diamond among guides took us to our hotel so we could cool off, both figuratively and literally, promising to pick me up at first light.

Broome is not over-endowed with hotel rooms – in fact Broome is not over endowed with anything except birds – so we found ourselves in a basic, clean hostelry. We saw that we would be able to eat and sleep in reasonable comfort, but it was not the sort of place from which you steal the bathrobes and toiletries – mostly because there were none of either. Had the temperature ever dropped, we would have been fine, because we had nice big woolly jumpers that we had worn as we set out on a chilly New Zealand Spring morning. Actually, the temperature never went below 30 degrees Celsius, even at night. Luckily we had carried our optics in our hand luggage, so we would be able to pursue the main reason for being here. In fact, the optics were the bulk of the hand luggage – but I was also equipped to take photos, read, clip my toenails and put on my eye shadow and lippy. However, as we had never fallen fowl of the lost luggage gremlin before we had not taken any precautions against loss – these days my hand luggage always includes a set of underwear and a fresh polo shirt. So, what had been sticking to our skin for the last 36 hours was all we *could* wear until Qantas deigned to route our luggage the intervening few thousand miles.

The temperature outside was well over 40 degrees and the relative humidity, although I didn't understand how this was possible, apparently 110%! We debated what to do and decided an early night made sense, so we washed our underwear and went to bed. Over many years of travel this had been our habit… wash your undies before going to bed and the air-con will dry them overnight. This way you can travel lighter and do not have to carry a bag full of dirty washing around. Not in this part of the tropics my friends! I awoke to find my pants were as wet as when I had gone to bed! There were but two options – go 'commando' or wear wet knickers. Not wanting to frighten the horses, nor add chafing to our sea of troubles, I went for the wetter option.

Out of compassion (and perhaps a hint of guilt at getting us into this situation) I took it upon myself to rearrange Maggie's smalls to take full advantage of the light from the high windows as well as the blast from the air-con. On my return to the room many hours later I found that the situation had not improved underwear wise… there was just no way anything would dry in Broome's sultry air.

The birding and George's guiding were terrific, and we had some superb days out. Highlights included being almost within touching distance of a Jabiru while we were stung multiple times by huge ants, a wonderful Scarlet-headed Honeyeater when squelching through knee-deep mud in mangroves, and finding an incredibly dull Mangrove Gerygone.

Maggie, re-energized after a mere 14 or 15 hours sleep, joined me after the first day. It took three days for our cases to re-join us, by which time I had washed my shirt twice, each time wearing it until it approached dryness. My thinking was that even if I started out dry in the morning I would become a soggy mess smelling like a wet dog as soon as I ventured forth – so I might as well be soggy but clean and smelling of Qantas soap! You might be wondering whether that sad and lonely Zebra Finch mentioned earlier was the only bird rearing its plumed pate in this piece? Of course not, would I short-change you?

Our final day in the company of George was spent, replete with the luxury of fresh clothes, in the search for some of the commoner species we hadn't yet encountered. At one point we had stopped near a tiny church besides a small freshly ploughed field. Across the field a mixed finch flock was picking its way along, while hunting out weed seed. Occasionally a group would take flight, 30 or 40 finches fluttering together.

Zebra Finches must be one of the most commonly kept cage-birds in every corner of the globe, but it is only in their natural habitat, such as this corner of a field, that they are at their best and certainly a small flock is where they belong, not in pairs behind bars! I suppose I can just about understand why people want to be so close to such little beauties, but this is where they belong, tiny balls of striped feathers, free to feed and fly and delight my eye.

Holding up the T-shirt it became apparent that Qantas™ believed all their passengers to be anorexic elves. Had I been able to get the T-shirt over my head it would have barely have become a self-respecting cravat…

Other birding books by Brambleby Books

Arrivals and Rivals – A duel for the winning bird
Adrian Riley
ISBN 9780954334796

UK500: Birding in the fast lane
James Hanlon
ISBN 9780954334789

Winging it – Birding for Low-flyers
Andrew Fallan
ISBN 9780955392856

The Ruffled Edge – Notes from a Nature Warden
Pete Howard
ISBN 9781908241061

Birduder 344 – A life list ordinary
Rob Sawyer
ISBN 9781908241092

Scilly Birding – Joining the madding crowd
Simon Davey
ISBN 9781908241177

www.bramblebybooks.co.uk